RUGBY FROM THE FRONT

Rugby From The Front

Peter Wheeler

Stanley Paul
London Melbourne Sydney Auckland Johannesburg

To Margie, Mum and Dad for their
encouragement and patience at all times

Stanley Paul & Co. Ltd
An imprint of the Hutchinson Publishing Group
17–21 Conway Street, London W1P 6JD

Hutchinson Group (Australia) Pty Ltd
30–32 Cremorne Street, Richmond South, Victoria 3121
PO Box 151, Broadway, New South Wales 2007

Hutchinson Group (NZ) Ltd
32–34 View Road, PO Box 40–086, Glenfield, Auckland 10

Hutchinson Group (SA) Pty Ltd
PO Box 337, Bergvlei 2012, South Africa

First published 1983
© Peter Wheeler 1983

Set in Baskerville by Tradespools Ltd, Frome, Somerset

Printed and bound in Great Britain by
Anchor Brendon Limited, Tiptree, Essex

ISBN 0 09 154660 5

Acknowledgements

I would like to thank David Hands, rugby correspondent of *The Times*, for all the work he has done in the preparation of this book. I have known David since 1971, when he first came to work on the *Leicester Mercury* and few journalists know more about the Leicester club than he, since he wrote the centenary history which the club published in 1981. He was the natural person to turn to when it was first suggested that I might write a book about my rugby career; he was also a constant source of interest to my sons, Ben and Tom, whose 'voices off' provided the background to many of our tape-recorded conversations. David left Leicester in 1978 to join *The Times* but his interest in the club's progress has been maintained. In other circumstances we might have shared each other's company in New Zealand in 1983, but I was not selected for the Lions and David's employers decided against sending their correspondent on the tour – which was my good fortune!

PHOTOGRAPHIC ACKNOWLEDGEMENTS

For permission to reproduce copyright photographs, the publishers would like to thank Colorsport, All-Sport, Neville Chadwick Photography, the *Citizen*, *South China Morning Post*, Mike Brett Photography, Jan Hamman, Colin Elsey/Colorsport, Adrian Murrell/All-Sport, *Daily Express*, Midland Press Agency and *Leicester Mercury*

Contents

Introduction

It may seem an obvious remark with which to open an autobiography, but life takes some curious twists and turns. Fifteen years ago I was living in a quiet London suburb: Peter John Wheeler, novice insurance broker, making his way through the comparatively tranquil pools of old boys' rugby. At the same age a certain Gareth Owen Edwards had played his first game for Wales. The mountains I was to climb were not even visible from the lowly rugby foothills among which I was scrambling.

Maybe it is all a question of opportunity, to release the ambition which lurks within us all. In my chosen sport I have known the heights of triumph, the valleys of failure. Rugby has been the means for me to express myself and more; it has given me insights to people and places which I hardly knew existed when I left school. It has been an education in the broadest possible sense and it has given me the happy chance to set down in this book the pleasure and the pain of learning. If, in doing so, I criticize the way the world of rugby is organized, it does nothing to lessen my delight in occupying that world.

When I sit down and reckon up what rugby has given me, it is the people I remember. The places I have visited read like a travel agent's catalogue but it is the people in those places who made them memorable. Whether it is exotic Hong Kong or Fiji, bustling Tokyo or homely Timaru, the rugbymen there are just the same – the language they talk is the same, the welcome they give you the same.

If you are successful in sport, total strangers begin to take an interest in your life, in your work, in your family. They 'know' you because they have seen you play, either in the flesh or on television, and many of them realize that underneath the white shirt with the rose on it, away from the roar of 60,000 voices at Twickenham, there is someone much the same as themselves.

What moments there have been. England's grand slam of 1980 encompassed the best and worst of Rugby: the rank, over-emotional display purveyed by England and Wales at Twickenham, the vivacity of the Calcutta Cup match at Murrayfield. I have been lucky enough to live in a city and be captain of a club that was good enough to win three cup finals and to be described, rightly or wrongly, as the best in the country. I could have put the same amount of work into playing for a club which never won anything. I played regularly against the most famous invitation club in the world, the Barbarians, and enjoyed myself playing for them. I have played thirty-six times for my country while playing for my club with men who put just as much effort into their game but did not play once for England. I made two tours with the British Lions and made lasting friendships with players and followers of the game in New Zealand and South Africa, as well as the leading players from Scotland, Ireland and Wales.

No one could easily walk away from a game that gives so much, yet rules which I regard as archaic have forced players to do so. It may be that the way I choose to be involved in rugby will disbar me from putting back into the game what I would want to. It remains to be seen if, once I am no longer good enough to play in Leicester's senior side, I will be able to play in the club's second or third team, helping youngsters learn the game the way so many people took the trouble to help me. At this stage I find it difficult to be sure where my career may take me once my playing days are over but I should love to continue to help Leicester in any way possible.

They have been, and I am sure they will continue to be, one of the great clubs.

You will find from this book that rugby's authorities and I have not always been in complete accord. My views on the game have been shaped by my upbringing and my playing experience and they are not shared by many of those who administer the game in England, nor possibly by many followers of the game. We each have our own ideas of what is best for the game. But it has been a good life. In the private world which all front-row players are said to occupy, I have taken a few balls against the head, both on and off the field. It has been as much as anyone could have wished for.

1

Out of the Pride

I was in the middle of the Irish Sea suffering from a hangover when the 1983 Lions party to tour New Zealand was announced. To be slightly more accurate, Margaret, my wife, and I were returning by ferry from Dun Laoghaire to Holyhead on the Monday following the Ireland–England match and I knew already that I was not in the party. I had deliberately arranged to be out of contact because speculation concerning the party had been intense throughout the international season with the added problem that both Cieran Fitzgerald, the captain of Ireland, and I were being suggested as likely candidates to lead the tour party. All things considered I felt that if I were lucky enough to be asked to captain the Lions, there would be plenty of time for cameras flashing and telephones ringing after I had taken it in. By the same token, if I was to be overlooked, I wanted time to gather my thoughts together before the inevitable deluge of calls and commiseration.

But it was not the captaincy issue which was so desperately disappointing as the fact that I was not in the party at all. It had been a conscious decision on my part the previous year to aim for the tour. Back in 1980 when the Lions ran on to the field for the fourth Test against South Africa in Pretoria, I thought I was playing my last game in a Lions jersey and worked harder than ever to make it a memorable occasion. Circumstances suggested that growing family and business commitments might prevent me from making another tour three years later, but circumstances changed and by the summer of 1982 I realized that I would be physically able to tour, that I wanted to tour – which is important – and that I had Margaret's backing and also that of my firm. It seemed, too, a happy way of rounding off my playing career.

The captaincy did not come into it, despite press speculation. I had always thought that Billy Beaumont, who did a wonderful job as captain of the 1980 Lions, would be in the frame again. Then, after injury forced Billy to retire in 1982 and Steve Smith became captain of England, I began to look at the other candidates, all of whom seemed to be dropping by the way. Andy Irvine, Scotland's captain and fullback, was forced out by injury and Jeff Squire, the Welsh flanker who had previously captained his country, was not available. Before the season ended he had been persuaded to change his mind and I thought then that he might be a very 'live' contender to captain the party. I would have been happy in any side he led, having toured with him in 1977 and 1980 and having developed considerable respect for his talents – he could always have reckoned on my support – but still the arguments in press circles seemed to revolve around Fitzgerald and me. Even so, I realized throughout the whole period that there was no substance to the stories. No one extracted anything from the tour manager, Willie John McBride, or the coach, Jim Telfer, so I never got carried away with anything I read in the papers.

But there was another element to fuel ambition, the competitive element which glows within all international players. I was the reigning Lions hooker; I had played in the last seven Lions internationals, three in New Zealand and four in South Africa, and now it was being suggested that another hooker would take my place. It was in no way an arrogant assumption on my part that the place was mine by right, because no player can ever assume that – even at club level. But it was just the challenge I needed to spur me on. The only response possible was to try and win selection for a third Lions tour and keep the Test place. I felt, too, that while there had been many problems for the Lions in New Zealand in 1977, I had always wanted to go back there because that tour had been a personal highlight. I felt I played there as well as at any other time in my career and many individuals had treated me kindly – it might have been a nice way to say farewell.

Yet there we were, ploughing north-east up St George's Channel, literally and metaphorically all at sea. The preparation and the match itself in Dublin, which England lost, had left a lot to be desired but Margaret and I had enjoyed a superb Sunday with friends, knowing by then that all decisions regarding the tour party had been made and there was nothing more anyone could do to influence them. Nevertheless I saw little point in prolonging the agony more than was necessary, so I made arrangements to ring Ian Robertson, then rugby correspondent of the *Sunday Times*, first thing on Monday morning. Ian himself was to procure the names of the party in advance of the official announcement, so it was with a distressing hangover that I stumbled out of my hotel bed to ring him at home. It was he who broke the news that Fitzgerald would be the captain and that Colin Deans of Scotland would be the second hooker. He went through the thirty names and we talked for ten minutes, but I was not taking in anything he said. From the jumble of thoughts churning around, two points finally emerged: one, that I was not going and the other, that the competition was over and that I had lost, which had happened to me very seldom as a player. It was like the feeling that comes after a long, hard game, when you have given your all but yet find yourself on the losing side when the whistle goes.

A subdued Mr and Mrs Wheeler made tracks for the nine o'clock ferry. The sea was extremely rough and I survived on two glasses of soda water at lunchtime. Several people who had been across to Dublin for the game passed by and offered best wishes for my tour prospects, not knowing the party had already been chosen. The good wishes turned to condolences when I

told them I would not be going and after a while I
stopped telling wellwishers that I already knew the party
– it was kind of them to think of me but it was far easier,
as far as I was concerned, to pretend ignorance. I had a
bad head and all I wanted to do was sit by myself rather
than go through ultimately embarrassing conversations
with strangers. In situations such as this you tend,
selfishly, to think only of yourself; a touch of self-pity
steals up on you. But by the time we reached Holyhead
and were on the long drive to Leicester, I was managing
to get matters into perspective. In the car there were long
periods of silence ... every so often, Margaret told me
afterwards, I would emerge from thought and say 'Oh
well...' and then relapse into gloom. My mother had
been looking after our two boys, Ben and Tom, over the
weekend and when we got home there were a few tears.
In some ways it was harder for Margaret and my
mother. I had known all along exactly what was
involved, that selection might not go my way. My family,
reading so many stories in the papers written by people
who felt I would go, could hardly fail to be influenced by
them so the final decision came as more of a shock.

I went down to the Leicester clubhouse that evening,
for regular Monday training. After a disappointment
such as this, one of the best palliatives is to get back
among the lads, the players from your own club, do some
work together, have a few pints. One or two will start
cracking jokes about all the gardening you can do in a
free summer and you begin to realize that, after all, it is
not the end of the world. Also I wanted to have a word
with Paul Dodge. In my opinion he has been the best
centre in the world for some seasons and he had not been
chosen for New Zealand either. He is not only a great
player, he is a great person to have around, on or off the
field. He was twenty-five, at the peak of his career. The
tour would have been just right for him. He had been a
Lion in 1980 but only as a replacement. He deserved to
be an original selection in 1983. He deserved to go far
more than I because he was so far ahead of the rivals for

15

his position in terms of ability, compared with my own situation. He was down at Welford Road too, training faithfully: Mr Reliable.

There was still time that day for a post-mortem at my local public house, in Rothley. By that stage I had begun to accept the decision and to start thinking about all the family's contingency plans for the summer. There is always another side to the coin, there has to be, even though it may not always feel like it. During eleven years of marriage, rugby had claimed a share of the summers as well as the winters. Now there was a prospect of giving back some time to Margaret and the boys which had previously been denied them. Diplomacy suggests a mention of my employers, who had given me so much paid leave of absence in the past and were now entitled to a much greater presence from P. Wheeler during the summer months. It would be difficult to exclude games completely but it had long been my ambition to get my golfing handicap of 23 down; it is wonderful what frustrations can be released on a little dimpled white ball. I had already received several offers to write a book; in accepting one of them I had not really considered how the book might be completed if I was wending my way through New Zealand. Now I could give that project proper thought and, at the same time, bring joy to Margaret's face by making inroads into boxes and boxes of cuttings and mementoes which have been gathering dust in a spare room in our home at Ragdale.

No, time would not lie heavily, though my immediate task the following day was to face the press (though not literally). With so many journalists having boosted my chances there was bound to be an inquest, but I had the impression that some of those who contacted me for my reaction would have preferred bitterness or anger. I felt nothing like that at all. So many things had gone my way in the past in terms of selection that I could hardly complain when one did not. I could not feel angry at something which had given me so much pleasure and I certainly could not hope that the tour would be a failure

16

just because I was not on it. I wanted none of the chosen
players to suffer the disappointments and frustrations the
1977 Lions had gone through. My feelings were those of
a replacement for an international match – a mixture of
emotions which is hard to appreciate unless you have
actually been in that position: a desire for the team to do
well but for the person playing in your position to play
just a little less than well, so that you may get your
chance. In fact I was carded to remain on stand-by
during the summer, which makes the replacement ana-
logy particularly pointed.

I was surprised and grateful during the weeks that
followed that so many people, many of whom I had never
met, took the trouble to write or telephone to express
their disappointment that I had not been chosen. Some
of them expressed themselves in quite emphatic terms.
An anonymous Welshman from Dinas Powis summed up
the feelings of most of them in a brief letter thus: 'I am
your average bigoted, short-sighted, partisan, cocky,
unknowledgeable and anti-English fanatical rugby sup-
porter and I think that the Lions selectors have even
outshone me in not picking you.'

Apart from Leicestershire there seemed to be pockets
of support in Essex and Sussex. Geoffrey Windsor Lewis,
secretary of the Barbarians, took the trouble to write and
invite me to join the annual Easter tour to Wales. It was
a gesture I appreciated and I was sorry I could not
accept. I had a typical letter from Andy Ripley, superstar
and former England number eight, who was somewhere
in Luxembourg at the time, and there was a telegram
from the Vigo club in Kent which said simply: 'We
grieve for you.' All the letters and messages showed
concern not only for me but for the state of the game
generally in Britain. I can only take it as a healthy sign
when so many people show how deeply they feel for the
game. To all of them my grateful thanks, though not to
the junior club from the south of England, one of whose
members rang me up and invited me to speak at their
annual dinner, which coincided with departure day for

17

the Lions. It seems his club had asked John Finlan, England's representative on the Lions selection committee, to speak and he had declined because of the farewell party for the Lions. He had passed on my name as a possible substitute, on the basis that I would be free of tour commitments. It was not a suggestion I welcomed and I had little compunction in turning the invitation down. The wound was still a trifle sore.

2

Analysis of a Tour

It would be unnatural if, at some stage after receiving a severe disappointment such as the tour decision, you did not sit down and try to analyse what went wrong. I did not feel let down. I believed that McBride and Telfer would insist upon having the two best available players for each position and that therefore they regarded me as being behind Fitzgerald and Deans. What others believed to be the case in relative rankings simply did not come into it.

It was always going to be a difficult tour. I knew of New Zealand players, like Murray Mexted, the number eight, who had been setting out their stall a year in advance to make sure of selection against the Lions in 1983. The players who went from Britain had to be the best available, to suit whatever game plan the management wanted to operate and I was sure that McBride and Telfer, both men whom I respect greatly, would cut through any political considerations which invariably bedevil these occasions and go for the players they believed would do the job they wanted.

No one has a divine right to selection. You offer yourself up, at whatever level. In the same way some players have consciously restricted their level of activity: Ray Gravell, the Llanelli and Wales centre, was a prime example of that during the 1982–83 season when he retired from international rugby yet, by all accounts, played exceptionally well at club level. Phil Bennett, captain of the 1977 Lions, did exactly the same before retiring altogether. Such players set their own standards, free from any expectation that their country will call on them.

But if you do offer yourself for international selection in a Lions year, then your form has to be so good that you virtually force yourself on to the tour. My form in 1983 was not that good. Moreover I was well aware that, whatever may have been said in the papers, the captain of the most successful side in the four home countries was going to be favourite to captain the Lions. History shows you that. It is ironic to think that, if injury had not forced Billy Beaumont to retire prematurely from the game, my prospects for New Zealand in 1983 might have been enhanced. Billy did a wonderful job of leading the Lions in 1980 and was a hot tip to be the first man to lead the Lions on two tours. Had he continued playing England's fortunes might not have been so mixed and Fitzgerald, Deans, Billy James of Wales and I might have been considered purely as hookers, without any question of captaincy clouding the issue.

But Billy had gone and I knew I was most unlikely to captain England. So when Fitzgerald added a shared championship to the triple crown and championship that Ireland had won in 1982, he was in the pound seats for the Lions job. The only time McBride and I were associated in the management of a team was in South Africa in 1982, when a five-nations party played three matches to celebrate the opening of the rebuilt Ellis Park stadium in Johannesburg. Syd Millar, the Lions manager in 1980, managed that party and McBride was the coach, at a time when he knew already that he was to manage the 1983 Lions and would have been directing his thoughts towards New Zealand. Fergus Slattery, another Irishman, was the tour captain, but I led the side that played Western Province in the second match of the brief tour and lost 42–6. It was not the most impressive credential I had to offer as a captain, whatever else I may have offered as captain of Leicester over five seasons.

The circumstances leading up to that particular game

could hardly have improved my rating. I had agreed with Syd that I would have to spend one day in Durban on business for my firm, and the most convenient day was the Sunday after the first match, against Transvaal. I was to fly back from Durban to Cape Town early on the Monday, in time for training. Monday, however, turned out to be the day on which all schools in Cape Town began again after the winter holidays and all flights south were overbooked. I spent all Monday at the airport and the only way I could get to Cape Town was via Johannesburg, which meant I would miss the training session in preparation for the game with Western Province. That alone would have upset the management but what made it worse was that, when I finally settled into my seat in the aircraft and picked up a paper, I was shocked to discover that I was to captain the side. There had been no inkling from the manager or coach so I spent the flight working out what to say to the team. Landing in Cape Town that evening I went straight to a team meeting at the hotel.

An added complication was that Maurice Colclough, the England lock, had only been able to join the party on the Sunday and that he and Donal Lenihan of Ireland, the chosen locks, were both used to packing on the same side of the scrum. With me missing from training we had done no line-out practice and all we managed in that area was half an hour the next morning in the hotel car park. In the afternoon we went out against Western Province and let in seven tries, all of them converted. They were the best provincial side in South Africa at the time but, not content with an established reputation, they brought in five guest players. We were crushed up front, pushed all over the field. Even if the Lions had played that side in the middle of a tour they would have done well to win; seven days in the middle of June was emphatically not the right preparation.

The previous evening, following the team meeting, McBride had come to my room to discuss aspects of the Western Province match. We wound up talking about

21

the Lions tour to come and how much the players were looking forward to it. McBride has always been a player's man, eager to discover as much as he can about individuals he is unable to watch regularly, to meet them directly, and obviously he was out to improve his background knowledge of potential English tourists. I hinted that some players I knew – not only Englishmen – were worried about the rumours regarding Telfer's training methods. I was aware from past experience that when the rain is pouring down in New Zealand and you are halfway through a long tour, there comes a time to slacken off the reins, that training every day is not always the answer.

Equally I was aware that someone like Telfer would be needed on tour, who would crack the whip when it was needed rather than being easy on players. Nevertheless I felt it was worth making the point to McBride so that he, in turn, while talking to players, would be able to reassure them or impress upon them the need for the Telfer approach – it could have made the difference between some experienced players making themselves available to tour or not. McBride would also have passed on my comments to Telfer who may have got the impression that neither I, nor some other Englishmen, were particularly keen on a hard summer's training, however far from the truth that may have been. Indeed Telfer was quoted as saying at a meeting with the press early in 1983 that he had heard one or two Englishmen were not looking forward to his methods. That could have been a black mark against me as far as the Lions coach was concerned. It may even have caused the management to wonder whether I might not be some kind of disruptive influence. Funnily enough the thought occurred to me that summer in South Africa that McBride might have been cast in the wrong role for New Zealand, he was such a good coach. Even though we had been through a hard domestic season in 1981–82 we trained every day in South Africa and hardly noticed it.

Overall, however, that was the only direct impression

of me as captain that McBride had to go on and he could hardly be blamed for thinking little of it. If I had captained England successfully since, I might have erased that impression but the opportunity did not arise. Indeed, England's poor 1982–83 season put a damper on other people's hopes besides mine. We began the season as many pundits' favourites for the championship but circumstances changed drastically between our return from the North American tour and the onset of the championship. We lost Phil Blakeway from the front row when he retired; we were without Clive Woodward at centre for three of the four games while he was restored to full fitness following an operation on his shoulder; and Colclough lasted only half a game. That was three world-class players out and another, Mike Slemen on the wing, was not even given a trial, though there proved to be no adequate replacement. This is not to decry the players who replaced them. They never let England down but none of them was in quite the same class and that was bound to have an effect, particularly on the scrummaging. We were weaker among the forwards which was no help to my tour chances, nor to John Scott's or Steve Smith's. Those three positions – hooker, number eight and scrum half, are the ones most affected by a poor scrummage performance.

Nevertheless, you can still play well, even if the team overall has declined. But my own fitness was not all it might have been in the second half of the championship. I was fine against Fiji and against the French but I suffered an ankle injury playing for Leicester against High Wycombe in the John Player Cup in January, missed the international against Wales, and the ankle kept niggling away. It was one of those annoying injuries which leaves you able to play with the ankle strapped up but unable to do all the fitness work you should do. I could not go for the five-mile runs or do the sprint training I needed. The overall effect was that I went into the games against Scotland and Ireland not worried about getting through them but aware of having felt restricted in training. Any experienced international will tell you that among the criteria for performing well is the need to concentrate on the game in hand rather than going onto the field pondering aspects of physical fitness. I came through both internationals feeling I had done my job but no more than that. It was not enough. You cannot leave anything to chance, you must put yourself into a position where you cannot be ignored in a Lions year.

I did not feel in any of them that I was outplayed. I could do the bread-and-butter basics that a hooker needs to do at international level without problem: I could throw the ball in, I could scrummage (which is 90 per cent of the hooker's game), I could tackle, I could tie up the blind side of rucks and mauls, or the front of the line-out. It was the extra bits and pieces, which might occur only two or three times in a match, with which I had difficulty; these are the things that get you noticed and may form a crucial part in the build-up to a try, just as Deans showed in a Scottish score in Paris that season. The speed about the field, the contribution in handling movements which has always been an important aspect of my play, were missing. I could not argue with the selection of Deans for the 1983 tour. As his experience increased, he had developed into a good, all-round hooker; he had enjoyed a good season, he was fast and fit, and under Telfer's coaching he had tightened up the areas in which previously he was a bit loose. I had felt for a long time that whether Fitzgerald or I went, Deans would be the other hooker.

Morale too had declined among England's players. They had gone down to Wales early in February and become the first England team in twenty years not to lose at Cardiff. Smith had played much of the game with damaged ribs yet his reward, and that of the other halfback, Les Cusworth, was to find themselves dropped for the Calcutta Cup match. I was recalled after my ankle injury; John Horton, England's fly half during the grand slam year of 1980, was brought back after a two-year gap and a new cap, Nigel Melville, was named as scrum half. In the event Nigel was unable to play against Scotland because of injury, but instead of giving a first cap to Nick Youngs, who had been named as the official replacement, Smith was brought back after having been left out of the original squad for the match altogether. It was an amazing piece of selection and, to my mind, destroyed the credibility of the men who were supposed to be picking the best available England team. Scott had been asked to lead the side in succession to Smith and although he was not enjoying the best of seasons, a good finish in the championship could have lifted his tour prospects. But we lost to Scotland at Twickenham and, sitting with John that evening, I was able to reflect on how a few hours had turned his hopes upside down.

At the same time that we were losing at Twickenham, however, Ireland were going down heavily to Wales. Suddenly Fitzgerald's chance of leading the Lions had receded (if the newspapers were to be believed) and speculation on the captaincy grew in intensity. Many people, whose opinions I respected, told me they felt I had become front runner which made it difficult to view the whole matter objectively. I did not go along with all the arguments for and against, but I have to admit that when I heard McBride was coming to Leicester to watch our John Player Cup quarter-final against the Harlequins, I thought he might possibly want to talk about tour selection or the captaincy, having heard that the captain is sometimes notified in advance of the main party. There were plenty of other reasons for him to be there, of course, since there were half a dozen players in that match with a prospect of either touring or being a tour replacement. McBride puffed his pipe and kept his counsel.

England's international season was to end in Dublin and still the discussion raged. Around Leicester there was only one candidate for the job; Dublin on the Thursday before the match gave me an entirely different perspective. The Irish press, not unnaturally, stood

25

foursquare behind Fitzgerald and if ever I had been getting carried away, that brought me up short. Even so, one established member of the English press corps told me that evening that he had lunched with Willie John recently and understood that the captaincy was still open. From what was said subsequently, after the tour party was announced, it seems he may have been misinformed.

Circumstances had changed yet again after the Scottish match. Smith was gone again, Youngs was at scrum half and David Trick, very fast and very inexperienced, came into the problem position, left wing. Woodward was finally regarded as fit and displaced Huw Davies at centre. Fate continued to dog the squad however: Scott went to bed that Thursday afternoon with influenza and Budge Rogers, the chairman of selectors, said that if he was unfit, I would lead the side. I had only once been called upon to lead England – in Tonga in 1979 when Beaumont had an ear infection – so I threw myself into the job thinking it would be an interesting confrontation with the opposing hooker who was also Ireland's captain. Scott recovered but at that stage of the season it would have taken a Herculean effort to put England back on the rails and we lost, leaving ourselves at the foot of the championship table. The stage was set for the tour announcement two days later and the party read: Dusty Hare, Hugo MacNeill, John Carleton, Trevor Ringland, Roger Baird, Gwyn Evans, Robert Ackerman, David Irwin, Michael Kiernan, Clive Woodward, Ollie Campbell, John Rutherford, Terry Holmes, Roy Laidlaw, Staff Jones, Ian Stephens, Cieran Fitzgerald (captain), Colin Deans, Ian Milne, Graham Price, Steve Boyle, Maurice Colclough, Donal Lenihan (who was replaced by Steve Bainbridge before the tour began because of a strained hernia, though Lenihan finally joined the party as a replacement), Robert Norster, Jim Calder, John O'Driscoll, Peter Winterbottom, Jeff Squire, John Beattie, Iain Paxton.

There were few surprises. Steve Boyle, the Gloucester

lock and a good tourist, rode the luck that had taken him into the England side but Colin Smart, England's loose-head prop, and Dodge were overlooked. I could hardly criticize the choice of Fitzgerald as captain after what he had achieved with Ireland in the course of two seasons; it was his selection as a hooker that worried me. The one thing a hooker must do, at any level but particularly at international level, is win his own scrum ball. The odd put-in or two may bounce back or get kicked through but Fitzgerald, throughout his international career, has regularly lost one or two balls against the head. When you get down to Christchurch and play what may be the Third or fourth Test against New Zealand, and they get a heel against the head and score from it, two months' work may have gone up in smoke.

It may seem like the criticisms of a disappointed rival but such a comparatively small thing may be the difference between winning and losing a Test series. When I looked at the tour party completely objectively, my main hope was that a technical fault should not prove too dear. It was hard to forget that it was the Welsh tight forwards who had given Ireland a rough ride in their championship match at Cardiff, when Fitzgerald appeared to have difficulty throwing in at the line-out in a gusty wind. Apart from the hookers, four of the eight Lions tight forwards were Welsh and Fitzgerald had to win their approval as a player.

One point of which much was made but which I do not accept, was that there was no place for me on tour with Fitzgerald as captain merely because my presence might embarrass him. On any tour, but specially a Lions tour, you need competition for places. The greater the competition the better everyone will play and so long as the captain is playing well it does not matter how his number two performs. But it is the ultimate success of the tour which is of paramount importance. After the enormous amount of work put in by players and management, no touring party should lose a series because the captain is too proud to drop himself. Easy to

27

say, but I would have been prepared to drop myself at any level if I felt I had not been worthy of my place.

Critics may feel this is all very well, given hindsight and the knowledge that, in terms of Test results, the 1983 side were the worst Lions to visit New Zealand. Some chickens came home to roost in the first Test when Fitzgerald lost a couple of balls against the head and appeared to have problems at the line-out. But there is no satisfaction in seeing that happen. My criticisms of Fitzgerald as a player were written before the tour began. I am in no position to judge him as a captain, having never played under him, but I assume that he has considerable qualities of leadership.

Once the party was chosen, however, it was time for all criticism to stop and my interest in the results was exactly the same as that of any other rugby enthusiast in Britain and Ireland. It is a matter of history now that the series was lost but I do not think defeat was inevitable, even after the lamentable fourth Test defeat by 38–6. Judging from what I saw in English papers and from television, and knowing what I do of New Zealand conditions, it was obvious the Lions of 1983 were working hard and the defeat against Auckland in the second match was not significant in the context of the whole tour. There was time to recover before the first Test. The Lions may not have been playing as well as they hoped but they had only a short period in which to try different combinations, against consistently difficult opposition.

To ensure the success of the tour, however, the Lions had to win the first Test. I cannot say, at a distance, how much importance was attached to that result but the management must have viewed it in the same way as I do. In the event they lost 16–12, though the 13–12 scoreline at injury-time might have been a fairer reflection. They lost, and the All Blacks gained, a lot of line-out ball and two pieces of scrummage ball. Had the Lions won that possession they might have achieved greater control. It is hard to avoid the conclusion that such a quantity of possession may have had a crucial bearing on the result. The Lions did not take the one clearcut try-scoring chance they were offered. It was a game they could, and should, have won.

At that stage the Lions had been on the road for a month. The All Blacks were just getting their act together. If New Zealand had lost they might have considered a change of emphasis, possibly a change of players. They did make one change, which only restored a fly half, Wayne Smith, who had been kept out by injury. If the Lions had won the first Test and lost the second it would still have left them with everything to play for. But New Zealand were only going to get better after the first Test. They took the second Test and wrapped up the series in the bitter rain of Dunedin, before spreading their wings at Eden Park, Auckland.

It is unfortunate that the Lions had to play in their Test side three or four players lacking genuine Test calibre. If that sounds an odd thing to say of proven internationals, my own experience tells me that there is a definite step up in class from International rugby in our domestic championship to Test rugby. One of the great strengths of New Zealand rugby organization is the pressure they place on individual players, and they will identify with consummate skill the players most likely to bend under pressure during the game, which is at its strongest in and around the ball-winning areas. If bad ball gets passed down the line the effect of this pressure is broadened.

The Lions backs have been criticized, rather unfairly, since several were better recognized as defensive players who could block the centre of the field. They performed that duty well. If, however, the intention was to play a fifteen-man game, then the original selection of the party is cast in some doubt. Some of the best British backs at the running and handling game were left at home. Yet they did have some useful runners on the tour and they should have used them more effectively. Certainly they should have counter-attacked from fullback with more

29

eagerness as an alternative to the ten-man rugby they seemed set upon when they were never in the position of knowing they would get enough possession to play that style of game effectively. In that respect they were not helped by lax refereeing of the line-out and it took them too long to work out an answer.

There were the usual complaints of foul play from the management which slightly surprised me. Not that foul play took place but that the Lions reacted as they did. The one thing which never helps a touring side is to complain, about anything, no matter how hard that may be. Australians and New Zealanders will throw your complaints straight back at you and you will be labelled 'whinging Poms'. You have to take all the mud that is thrown, the kicks, the raking, the obstruction – the only effective answer is to win. The management may be seen as doing too little to defend their players but they must explain to the touring party why it is better to say nothing, and they must make the players understand. It is incredibly difficult to watch what you regard as illegality and dirty play taking place with your own players on the receiving end, but while the tour is still on you must accept it and the players must deal with problems on the field as they arise. Anyone who has toured in New Zealand must know what to expect and should have equipped himself with players who will stand no nonsense. It was, after all, Willie John whose 1974 Lions were supposed to have coined the '99' call.

It is the same for sides touring this country. It is a fact of modern tours that matches are becoming harder because sides are better organized, better prepared. In 1977 the Lions played twenty-five games; in 1980 they played eighteen and the 1983 Lions did the same. I think there is no doubt that the ten-week tour is here to stay and it may be, in that case, that tour organizers should consider reducing the number of Tests from four to three (slightly difficult for incoming tours when there are four home countries to be played). Financial considerations may suggest the number should stay at four and I would have thought that when you have the best players in the country at your disposal on tour, you should be able to sort out your Test side in four weeks. What can be done is to reduce the number of awkward midweek games, particularly in the week leading up to a Test match. New Zealand have always wanted to give their leading provinces a game against the tourists but it may be that in the future they will have to rotate fixtures from tour to tour. That has happened in Britain where sides who traditionally played the touring teams have had to relinquish their fixture in the interests of the visitors. The other alternative is to have a merger of sides but then you suffer a loss of identity. Certainly I could sympathize with Willie John at having to play Canterbury the Tuesday before a Test match.

I have no doubt that the 1983 Lions could have done little more in terms of preparation than they did. The difference between the two sides sprang from better planning on New Zealand's part, the identification of the Lions' strengths and weaknesses and the realization of how to reduce the one and magnify the other. They had two backs, Dave Loveridge and Steve Pokere, of infinite skill and they had discipline. Any side that can play through two Test matches which have the series hanging on them, and concede only one penalty within kicking distance of goal, has to be admired.

3

Streets of London

The wind and wet of Wellington, the sun-baked ground at Johannesburg are a long way from the milkman's round in South Norwood, the district in south London where I was born on 26 November 1948. It is not what you might describe as a strong rugby area nor were we a strong rugby family, though many of my relations were interested in sport. My father, Wally, was the eldest of a large tribe of Wheelers who came from that area while my mother, Margaret, came from Caterham in Surrey. I was the second of three sons; Frank, the eldest by some eighteen months, went on to play amateur football to a high standard, and when I was seven we were joined by David at our home in 71 Albert Road, South Norwood.

It would be nice to recall some graphic incident which inspired me to play rugby but there was none. Football was the game Frank and I played in the local park, and cricket in summer. Our house was a big, old semi-detached building, where we occupied the ground floor and another family the first floor, and there was enough garden for us to rag around in. If the park lacked appeal Frank and I had two other favourite 'playgrounds': the local cemetery where we would get into trouble as we tried to knock conkers down from the horse-chestnut trees and, lamentably, the sewage works. I doubt if we ever gave a thought to the basic functions of the works as we played leapfrog over the long revolving arms which sprinkle the coke in the distribution tanks. More usefully we sometimes joined my father, who worked for the local dairy, on the milk round with the horse and cart or jumped on our bicycles early in the day to do a paper round each.

The primary school which we attended was attached to St Mark's Church, just round the corner. The headmaster's name was R. C. Ives – which can leave no one in any doubt about what his nickname among the pupils was – and he did a splendid job organizing the football team in winter and the cricket team in summer. I seem to remember captaining both teams at one time or another from a position far removed from that which I played in rugby: I became goalkeeper, or sometimes right back, and usually played wicket-keeper on the cricket field. But ours was a small school and our opposition usually had more boys to choose from; consequently we seldom won though that did nothing to lessen the enjoyment when the team piled into Mr Ives's Austin A40 for an 'away' game. The memory remains vivid of one football match played on a miserably cold day, in pouring rain, on a pitch where there was a huge puddle in front of the goalmouth. The first time a shot came in I had to dive – crawl is probably more like it – through this puddle to try to stop it. My lack of success is indicated by the 0–13 scoreline against us.

The academic side of school appeared, initially, to present no problems, but when I moved up to John Ruskin Grammar School I found the homework getting in the way of football in the evenings. There was never any great pressure at home to be a brilliant scholar but, after only a year there, my father changed jobs to become the manager of a newsagent's shop in Crofton Park, Brockley, which is in south-east London. It was only some fifteen minutes away by car – not that we had one – but for me it was like moving to the other end of the world. Our new home was 63 Crofton Park Road and my new school was Brockley County Grammar School, where the game was rugby football. I was introduced most reluctantly to the game, not only because I had never played it but because my new form-mates had already had a year to get used to the tricks the strange-shaped ball could play.

There were compensations in the move, of course. We lived above the corner shop and it was then I must have acquired the habit I have never lost of wanting to read as many papers in the morning as possible. I'm lost without a newspaper. Not that it was the *Daily Express* or the *Mirror* which grabbed my attention then, it was the endless stream of comics which we would read, then replace on the counter. It was hard, too, to keep our grubby hands out of the jars of sweets – we didn't put those back. On the other hand, if your parents run a newsagent's, it's a bit difficult to avoid the paper round, or two rounds if one of the other boys failed to appear any morning.

Nor were we far from the rest of the family. There was always an uncle and aunt popping round – we were a close-knit bunch anyway – and some of my relations were genuine characters. One uncle, Derek, used to do a comedy singing act in the local clubs and everyone would get together for a huge party at Christmas, the high spot of the year for the children. Holidays were often taken as a group too, first of all at a Hastings guest house but subsequently at Madison's Holiday Camp, Littlestones, near Dungeness. If you have ever watched the television series, *Hi-de-Hi*, it was just like that, the chalets, the organized sports and entertainments. Later on the family made tracks for a caravan at Shanklin, in the Isle of Wight, where again we would have a litter of uncles to help in games of beach football and cricket.

Life, you will have gathered, was far from serious and far from dull. Nevertheless school persistently got in the way; during my first year at Brockley I would play rugby in the mornings on Saturday because I had to and football in a boys' club league in the afternoons. Then the rugy gradually took over, as I discovered more about it. I had the classic introduction to my position: at the first games session the master looked me over and said: 'Right, you'll play hooker.' All I was told was that whenever there was a scrum

34

it was my job to kick the ball backwards (yes, backwards) through the forest of legs for someone else to do something with. The French master was in charge of games that year and he had the wonderful habit of awarding penalties whenever anyone did something good. If you made a good tackle, your side was awarded a penalty. I never found that one in the laws. I was never more than average size – if I had been any bigger I might have found myself in the second row – and I never played in any other position, apart from the odd game at prop when there were too many hookers available.

I am not altogether sure how many of the boys knew exactly what they were supposed to be doing; I certainly did not when I was asked to run the line at an under-fifteen county match and I am sure the referee came to put little reliance on whether my flag was up or down. Even so I must have made some progress as a player because, in my fourth year, I went to the Kent schools trials and was invited to a training weekend at the Duke of York's School, Dover. That was my first 'solo' flight, as it were, since no one else from Brockley was involved. I was ordered to report for the weekend with track suit, training shoes, bits and pieces of equipment, none of which I had. So much of the world was still strange, certainly the rugby world. How different from Welsh boys of my age, growing up steeped in the history of the game, their own heroes to watch each week, the gifts at Christmas of a red rugby shirt or track suit for the luckier ones.

Any prospect of playing for the county disappeared when I caught glandular fever during my final year at school, which severely depleted my attendance not only at rugby but at all the other sports I enjoyed, the badminton, the cricket, the tennis. It might have been supposed that the enforced rest would have given me more time for study, but I left school with little academic distinction which is something I regret enormously now. I was not even aware that institutions such as St Luke's College, then famous as a centre for physical education and now part of Exeter University, or its Midland equivalent, Loughborough Colleges (now a university) existed. Knowing what I do now I am sure such a course of study would have suited me admirably but there was no one to point me in that direction. Examinations did not seem terribly important. There was plenty of employment so I followed the same road as many of my contemporaries and left school. My parents probably felt that was the next logical step and were happy to see me keeping (mainly) to the straight and narrow. I sometimes wonder what might have happened when I was sixteen if I had not caught glandular fever, had played during that season and perhaps made the county schools side. It might have encouraged me to believe there was something worth staying on at school for but, in the event, I took the trail to the careers advisor who, it seems to me, saw his function as fixing people up with jobs (which it largely was) without worrying too much about the nature of the person or the job. I told the advisor my examination passes and was sent to be interviewed by a firm called Gardner, Mountain, D'Ambrumenil and Rennie Ltd. Subsequent mergers produced Hogg Robinson Ltd, the international group of insurance brokers for whom I have always worked. They were prepared to offer me a three-month trial and so I started me on the life of a commuter, travelling up to the City every day as a trainee broker. Looking back, and comparing it with the difficulties which face youngsters coming out of school today, I can only consider myself exceptionally fortunate.

After two years as a trainee I progressed to the status of broker and became accustomed to transacting business at Lloyds. I enjoyed the work, I enjoyed meeting so many different kinds of people, learning how to suit policies to the requirements of the individuals or individual firms. I enjoyed earning a living. It was completely different from anything I had been used to before, a new world as I stepped down from the train and walked over London Bridge into the City. I had seldom given much thought at school to the day-to-day business of earning a

crust or whether a doctor earned more money than a
train driver. My colleagues then would probably say I
was very quiet, concealing the fact that there has always
been a strong sense of humour running through the
family. I think probably I had to be, to give myself a
chance to come to grips with a new social environment
and with working with people from all walks of life, many
of them considerably more moneyed walks than my own.

It took a lot of getting used to and, for a year, rugby
was forgotten. I had a girl-friend in Marylebone before
the urge eventually returned to look up some old school
friends, which took me along to the Old Brockleians
Rugby Club. It was no particular yearning to play rugby
again. I was not aware of having any great talent for the
game, and certainly I had no ambitions in rugby. I
began playing with the old boys as the answer to a social
need; where they played me, or for which team (they ran
five) was up to them. It had been much the same at
school when I played where I was told to and, having no
grounding in the game, assumed that the better players
were placed in positions where they could score tries
more easily than I could.

I had watched no first-class rugby, apart from one
school visit to Twickenham to watch the University
Match, which was a day out for the lads with the rugby
being largely incidental. It was only after I had been
playing for the Old Brockleians for a while that one of the
other players congratulated me on being chosen for the
first team while we were both waiting for a train up to
London, and I realized that this was a game in which I
might start taking an interest.

Everyone needs a starting point; more often than not it
comes when you find some small success, as I did then. I
became more closely involved with the club's activities,
and the society and outlook I found there, in turn, had a
lasting influence upon me. It provided me with a
grounding to rugby which I lacked before and set certain
standards in my relationships. I would probably have
received the same 'education' in most other junior clubs;

one of the endearing habits of the Old Brockleians was that the senior members made sure that they paid for many of the drinks consumed by us younger men. They knew that we were just starting out, that our jobs did not bring us a big wage and that we could not afford to join in the sessions after matches. They helped us, happy in the knowledge that it had been done for them and that we, in turn, would do it for those who came afterwards. In those days, of course, there was nothing so civilized as dances and discos where wives and girl-friends could enjoy themselves rather than being regarded exclusively as providers of teas.

It was very much an all-male society and most clubs became identified with a particular pub and were famous for their own characters. Beginners like myself were frightened by stories of legendary players we were likely to meet in other old boys' sides and the horrible things they were likely to do to us on the field, or to other people off the field. Such legendary figures always knew every verse to every rugby song ever composed and we had one of our own at the Brockleians, a bachelor named Mick Cast, who must have been in his mid-thirties, who lived for the club. He was a prop forward, with short-cropped hair and an inexhaustible supply of funny stories.

It was his habit to take young players under his wing, tell them the club's history, encourage them as they developed, and help them out if they were a bit short of cash. He was an immensely generous man, particularly on Easter tour when the club always went to Torquay. He worked in a bank, lived in a flat by himself and, when he was not at the club, spent much of his time at the same pub in the Old Kent Road; many's the night after a match when the players would troop down to the pub with Mick and spend hours round the piano bawling out their favourite songs. Mick committed suicide while I was still playing for the old boys; it appeared that, despite his generosity, he had pressing financial problems. Immature as I was then, it still gave me an indication of how lonely people can be, even if they appear the most gregarious of individuals. Surely if he had possessed some close friends he could have talked the problem through, yet the church was packed for the funeral service. He, I am certain, would have derived great pleasure from my progress in rugby because he was always keen for me to do well and actively encouraged me to join a first-class club, which probably meant Blackheath as far as he was concerned. 'Go and try,' he would tell me. 'It's better to try and fail and come back to us, rather than spend the rest of your life wondering whether you might have made it. You'll always be an Old Brockleian at heart.'

He was right too. I've seen it all over the world. Basically the same type of person turns out for Old Brockleian fourths as plays for England, in that they get the same pleasure from the game at their different levels, and experience the same camaraderie off the field. I admit that, over the last few years, a slightly different type has come into the game, a smoother, more fashion-conscious type, but so many of us are the same, which enables me to identify very easily with players at the other end of rugby's scale. You see them in clubs up and down the country; those who play for England have a vast amount more skill, more dedication, a more competitive spirit, but take those things away and the personality beneath is the same. You can recognize them, even in a totally different setting. One of the best nights I ever had was on tour with England in Japan in 1971. Several of us, English and Japanese, sat down together for several hours – they could not speak our language, we certainly could not speak theirs, but the drinking, the singing, the sign language and the pidgin English brought us all close together. In some ways that may be part of a vanishing world, for it would be naive to think that changes at the top in rugby will have no affect on players lower down the scale. I believe it has happened in cricket where the attitude of players seen in Test matches on television is beginning to be reflected among the village cricketers: the appeals for lbw are growing, no one walks any more until given out. The more televised internationals you watch, the more chance you have of seeing many of the undesirable elements in rugby, and the greater the prospect of youngsters coming into the game imitating what they see.

Not that I was one to philosophize as a junior member of a London old boys' club. Ours was a typical clubhouse, which looks from the outside much the same now as it did in the mid-1960s. Our fixture list took in the likes of the Colfeians, Askeans, Shootershillians, Beccehamians, all the old boys' clubs in south-east London, and we were far from the most successful of those. Perhaps the biggest day in the club's life while I was there was our win in the Old Askeans sevens tournament. We had never before reached the final, let alone won it, but that success capped a better-than-average season and I first received an inkling that if you get your sums right on the field, everything else will follow – the functions become better attended, more people want to do something for the club.

The other event which stays in the memory, blurred perhaps at the edges, was the traditional Easter tour – coincidentally we used to play Plymouth Albion Extras on the afternoon of their first XV's morning game with Leicester – and that year of the Askeans sevens we went west and won both our tour games for the first time. Our tour headquarters was always the Forest Hotel in Torquay and, naturally enough, it was on tour that I first found myself genuinely the worse for wear – one of the wives who accompanied the tour told me the following morning that she had slapped my face for something I had said or done but for all that I could remember she could have branded me with a red-hot poker.

In my first season with the club I put on nearly a stone (which took me to the vast weight of 11 stone plus) which was a result of playing regularly and drinking equally regularly, though little enough of the extra weight was fat. I was growing – at seventeen, playing first-XV hooker I should hope I was – and I was learning about my position. We had a couple of reasonable props but coaching was in its infancy and I picked up bits and pieces as I went along. It was like that throughout my three years with Old Brockleians and during my last year with the club I was picked for Kent's second XV, playing games against Eastern Counties seconds and Middlesex county clubs. Both the club and the county officials were talking of the possibility of first-class rugby for me at the end of that season and I dare say that, had I stayed, I would have taken their advice and joined Blackheath. I had given no thought to the first-class game, merely accepted selection for a county team as a pleasant surprise, but then my firm administered a jolt to my comfortable rut.

Hogg Robinson, like many other businesses at that time, were finding themselves premises outside London and they were keen to install a computer and move many of the processing staff to Leicester to develop the computer programme. Initially I was not involved until the firm decided the new department needed someone with my sort of experience. When the suggestion was put to me I was surprised; I had only a sketchy idea of where Leicester was. I had, after all, hardly been north of Watford. But there were advantages to a young bachelor such as myself: there was a disturbance allowance of 30 per cent of my annual salary, tax free, with no long-term commitment. That, I thought, would buy me a car and in six months I would be back in London, with another company if not with Hogg Robinson because the job market, in my field, was quite open then. At the age of twenty I had it all worked out so, in March 1969, I moved to digs in Leicester; I travelled up and down the M1 for the rest of that season, playing for the old boys and bearing a tide of dirty laundry to my mother. I would return on the Sunday night, with clean gear and perhaps a home-made steak and kidney pie; that was one habit I learned from life at home, the appreciation of good food.

4

The Tigers' Lair

I had no idea what I was joining when I became a member of Leicester Football Club. Tradition, you will remember, had played little part in my rugby career and I was completely unaware of the club's long and distinguished history. I had little leisure for finding out either; I was living in a flat in Imperial Avenue, off the Narborough Road, with two of my colleagues from work, all of us busily involved in establishing the company's new office in Vaughan Way. We worked long hours but it made a distinct change from London to go out of the office in the evening with colleagues, male and female, for a drink or a meal together. In London we commuters had headed for the trains when the working day was done.

I did have time to track down the identity of Leicester's secretary, Jerry Day, and apply for membership of the club. It was impossible not to be impressed with Leicester's ground, the huge stands between the Aylestone and Welford Roads out of the city, the popular banks at each end. Only one of the banks remains now, the Aylestone Road end having been flattened to give additional clubhouse facilities and car parking. I trained hard during the summer of 1969, sitting in my corner of the dressing room and eyeing the better-known players – and also the rival hookers, of whom there seemed to be far too many. Odd though it may seem now, Leicester had no current international players at that time, though there were many players with a wealth of experience, one of whom, Kevin Andrews, was the captain during the

1969–70 season. He awarded me the nickname of 'Hopsack' (the inevitable penalty of coming from Kent) though I later acquired another, 'Wheelbrace' (or just 'Brace'), which I received from the Coventry and England centre, Chris Wardlow, on tour with England in 1971.

The first-team hooker was John Elliott, an England trialist who later became a Midlands selector, and there were four of us hoping to stake a claim to a place in the Extras or the Swifts, Leicester's third team. I played my first game in Leicester colours for the swifts against Nuneaton thirds, though it was in the unfamiliar position of prop. It was much the same as old boys' rugby but I was relieved to be selected as hooker for my next outing, against Lutterworth – until I lost my first scrum against the head. Helped by some very experienced props, however, I settled down and it was a rewarding day when the club had their three hookers selected for county championship games, John Elliott for Notts, Lincs and Derby, Richard Berry, son of the former Rugby Union president Tom Berry, for Leicestershire and me for Kent. County rugby was just right for me then, playing with many other hopefuls and one or two old heads, and Kent did well, urged on by enthusiastic officials such as Alex Hemming, until recently the county's representative on the Rugby Union. We lost by only 22–17 to a Surrey side containing several internationals and beat Middlesex – J. P. R. Williams and all – by 9–6. It was not enough to get us into the semi-finals but it was a good season, ending against Hampshire, which coincided with my twenty-first birthday. It was typical of the county officials involved that they organized an evening for the county squad at the end of the championship season at a pub on the Thames at Greenwich. Since it was my birthday, I wound up in a completely paralytic state.

But at the club I was still finding my way around. I was content with my place in the Swifts, hoping for the odd game with the Extras, scarcely dreaming of a place in the first team, so it came as a shock when, at training the week before the game against Cambridge University, Andrews told me I was to play in the firsts. I had not realized that Elliott would be required as a replacement for Midland Counties (East) against the touring South Africans; Berry was injured so the place was mine, against a university side which included another England trialist hooker, Phil Keith-Roach. With several of our regulars required for the Springboks match, 8 November 1969 was not a particularly auspicious day and we lost at Cambridge 36–11. We all went to the Hawks Club afterwards and watched on television the Midland XV losing 11–9 at Leicester, which gave me the chance to appreciate the play of some of the men I had seen training at Leicester earlier in the week. They were massive men, those Springboks, or they looked like it to me as I sat at the bar and watched them.

I had a handful of first-team games that season as I gathered in experience from every side. There was my first visit to Wales, when I begged a place on the coach going down to Stradey Park where we were to play Llanelli. I went as a reserve and watched Leicester crash 43–11, a game in which Bob Rowell, the England lock who returned to the club that season, was sent off. It was enough to sit there and let the surge of Welsh excitement and emotion ebb and flow around me – no visitor to Stradey can fail to appreciate it. Rodger Arneil, the Scotland and Lions flanker, joined Leicester that season and there were other newcomers like myself – Robin Money, a fullback from Jordanhill, Bleddyn Jones, a fly half from Ammanford, David Pickering, another Scot and a hooker. All of us were young men needing encouragement in the game and David, Robin and I were able to offer each other mutual encouragement when we shared a house together. Robin broke that party up when he became engaged.

When I joined Leicester there was an immediate sense of identity, of belonging to a particular city and county, which London clubs often lack. A major factor in the development of Leicester as one of the country's leading clubs was the work in the early 1900s of Tom Crumbie, the secretary for over thirty years, and I quickly came to understand that it was the kind of club which attracted outstanding personalities, both players and administrators. I do not believe that has changed since I have been there. The greatest change has been in the commercial conduct of the club, which is something the game as a whole has been coming to grips with (or not, as the case may be) during the 1970s. But all the ingredients for the success Leicester have enjoyed over the last five years – three John Player Cup wins, two losing finals, the reputation of England's champion club – were there in those early days, save for the addition of two or three outstanding players.

During my time at Leicester nothing has changed my conviction that success stems directly from what happens on the field of play. Tom Crumbie took the right direction before and after the First World War; he knew exactly what he wanted for the club and ran himself and his business into the ground achieving it. No administrator in the country did what Crumbie did for Leicester and the secretaries who followed him were, on the whole, men of equal stature and vision. But Crumbie made sure that the playing side was correct; he brought players from all over the country, he laid on special trains, he made them feel a sense of importance playing for Leicester. I would never suggest that he did anything that was not in the book – after all he was a member of the Rugby Union committee – but he had built a splendid ground and he knew how to fill it. Twenty to thirty thousand people turned up for matches in those days and, though there is no prospect of getting those numbers on a regular basis today, I have seen crowds increase from a miserable couple of hundred to the four or five thousand we see regularly now. Perhaps if we suffer a couple of unsuccessful seasons, some of these thousands would be off and away but not that many. So many more people and businesses have developed a direct interest in the club.

It is a very delicate balance to achieve, the weighing of interests of the players and of the members. There have been times when I felt the club committee got the wrong balance, because they were more concerned with facilities for those who paid their annual subscription rather than facilities for the playing of the game which is what any rugby club is formed to promote. Generally speaking though we have had sufficient numbers on either side of the fence to achieve the desired effect, some of them committeemen who are still actively involved in playing the game. The administration is there to make the resources available for the players to perform to the best of their abilities, and if you do that and success comes, the spin-offs are endless. Once we began to find playing success we found that courtships with local firms developed into firm engagements. Companies and their clients and staff would come down to watch the match they had sponsored and find themselves enjoying the atmosphere so much that they became regulars.

The gradual change in the standing of the club over the ten years between 1969 and 1979 was helped by the formation of an *ad hoc* committee in 1976 to take a long and critical look at the internal organization at Leicester and at what could be done to improve it. It was, if you like, a mini-Mallaby, only, unlike the Rugby Union who asked Sir George Mallaby and his committee to take a critical look at the whole English game in the early 1970s, we took some notice of the findings and instituted many of them. That came just before the club's successful period in the John Player Cup competition, when commercial activity rocketed, and went a long way towards helping us cope with the vastly increased administrative problems we had to face. But it is also pertinent that, at much the same time, the drills which Chalkie White, the club coach, had been hammering into us for several seasons began to bear fruit. Running the ball, developing new moves with the ball in the hand, does not just happen and you need players with the skill to do it properly. When I joined the club we had some

46

admirably sound players but none had the class of Paul
Dodge and Clive Woodward. Bleddyn Jones at fly half
was a good distributor of the ball; Les Cusworth was an
even better distributor. Without such players our at-
tempts to play consistently open rugby might have
foundered and we would probably have changed the
formula because, if success is not forthcoming, change is.

Unlike football clubs, of course, rugby cannot go into a
transfer market to find the right players, to create the
right chemistry. One must accept that some good players
have weaknesses in which case the coach makes sure that
they play as well as their ability allows. No player should
be asked to adopt a style of rugby of which he is
incapable. It might be said that we were lucky to have
someone like Chalkie, with his coaching ability, his
vision for the game and his high moral standing, but the
traditions and outlook of the club seem to attract that
kind of devoted person. I believe it has done so again
with Graham Willars, who succeeded Chalkie as coach
in 1983. Obviously other clubs up and down the country
have bags of character and a history which in some cases
is longer than Leicester's. It would be wrong for me to
claim anything special on Leicester's behalf because I
have only experienced as a visitor what other clubs have
to offer. But I do believe, arrogant though it may sound,
that we have a special, almost unique, atmosphere at
Leicester.

Part of that atmosphere derives from the way members
react to each other, be they first, second or third-teamers,
officials or anyone else. When we were struggling to
make ends meet in the early seventies an easy answer
was to abolish the third team, the Swifts, which had been
the source of endless argument and much bad feeling
between Leicester and local junior clubs since its foun-
dation in the mid-1950s. But I maintain that the Swifts
are almost the most important part of the club because
they help make it a club in the genuine sense of the word,
an organization to provide rugby for players of varying
standards, who can all derive the same pleasure from the

game. We stand or fall by such players. We must not become a transit camp for players who, though they may know they are not good enough for the senior side, play for five or six weeks then move on to tell some other club that they have played for Leicester. We have to be big enough to incorporate players of lesser ability while not becoming as vast as those clubs which run a dozen sides, where the first XV is necessarily remote from the twelfth XV. It is the lesser-known players who serve as a counterweight to the internationals in the first XV, who keep their feet on the ground. Because we at Leicester maintain a rota of duties in the club, such as bar duty which many first-class clubs have surrendered to part-time staff, it is difficult (though not impossible) for a them-and-us situation to develop. Swifts and youth-team members find themselves rubbing shoulders with regular first-teamers and both benefit from the experience.

The youth team too, which began in 1972, was a visionary exercise encouraged by Chalkie and by Jerry Day. It coincided with the period when the traditional feeding areas for rugby clubs, the old grammar schools, were beginning to feel the pinch exerted by the move towards comprehensive education. It was the best possible way of getting talented youngsters involved with the club and we were fortunate to have a good liaison with local teachers: it was two schoolmasters, David Lyons from Syston and Mick Death from Hinckley, together with a former county president, Joe Pickup, who put the youth on its feet and scoured England and Wales for fixtures. We needed such a team at a time when the feed from local junior clubs was poor and the relationship between Leicester officials and junior-club officials even poorer. Many looked upon us as poachers, a hangover from the days in the 1950s when we were still an invitation club, but some of the Leicester officials failed to rid themselves of the habit they had accepted as young men.

I have learned so much from the club. For example, it is very frequently the little things which make the difference between success and failure, those little things which most often go unappreciated by anyone except the players and those close to them but which must be attended to so as to create the best atmosphere. Take someone like Eric Lacey, president of the club during our centenary year. Eric played for the club as a lock; he is a big man, with a big moustache, always happy to speak his mind. He and his wife, Sue, helped bring Leicester into the 1980s as far as attitudes to wives and families were concerned. Instead of letting wives and girl-friends wait around in the car park while their menfolk changed he invited them into the president's room for a drink or a sandwich. I never believed, until Eric became president, that anyone in his position could have so much influence upon the outlook of a club.

Take the groundsman: Fred Cox occupied that position when I joined and he was very good. We went through a poor patch after his departure to a better-paid job with a seed company but then we found Derek Limmage, who is now accepted as one of the club characters to the extent that he is ritually thrown into the team bath at the end of each season. Take the team secretaries, such as Tudor Thomas. His own playing experience was very limited and there was a feeling at Leicester when the post of first-team secretary fell vacant that it should go to a distinguished former player, it was regarded as such a prestigious position. But Tudor got the vote and because of his enthusiasm, his willingness to work, his attention to detail, he has made a tremendous success of it. He keeps attendance records at training, details of players' weights and, as important, he is a sympathetic character whom the players feel they can talk to, a sounding-board if you like.

Take David Lishman, the membership secretary. Businesses would pay huge salaries for the sort of service he provides and yet he happily does it for nothing, wearing a slightly bigger smile than the computer which might, in other enterprises, carry out the same function. Take the two secretaries I have known, Jerry Day and

John Allen. No one could have put more hours into the club than Jerry, who was like Tom Crumbie in many ways, a man with his own business and an abiding love for Leicester Football Club. John, who was the scrum half when I joined the club, has a more modern style and delegates much more easily but is an exceptional organizer and a shrewd businessman. There are many others like them, all with a tremendous ambition on Leicester's behalf, and their attitude provides a breeding ground for their successors.

It would be wrong to forget the members entirely of course. They are the ones who seek a sense of involvement whether by watching or by offering their services in so many little ways. It took the club a long time to discover how much they wanted to help, if someone would only ask them. One of the penalties of our success has been the sheer logistical problem of accommodating everyone in the club room; so, to create more space for members and their friends, we have plans for a separate players' dining room, which many clubs have anyway. I hesitated about such a step. All players enjoy competing in front of big crowds – the adrenalin rises that bit more – and we enjoy the interest they take in us. Hitherto the players have always had their meal in the club room where they can chat with the members, where they can find common ground. You meet the parents and families of other players and get to know your club colleagues better as you discover much more about their backgrounds. I feel it is not entirely the right answer to put the members in one room and the players in another, however much necessity demands it, and I hope that if we tread that road at Leicester the players will always remember that the public deserve their share of the players' attention.

What about the players? I have known so many at Leicester: some whose names have become household words in the rugby world; some unknown outside Leicestershire and the columns of the *Leicester Mercury*, save for those annual visits at Christmas of the Barbarians which did so much to focus attention on the club, even when we were struggling. I could not possibly mention all I would like to but let me start with two back-row men who gave me so much help when I was a newcomer, David Matthews and Graham Willars. David played over five hundred games for Leicester and what he did not know about forward play probably wasn't worth knowing. He is a farmer, down-to-earth, says little but when he talks he cuts through all the rubbish and says what needs saying. He and Graham were a formidably intelligent pair of forwards, both of them unlucky not to receive higher representative recognition. They had, and still have, immense respect for each other and they elicited tremendous respect from the players around them, and that includes the opposition. They were both local men and played much of their rugby before I joined the club. Bleddyn Jones made his debut in the same season as I did and you could not help but admire him, a man blessed with exceptional humility and all the courage in the world. When he joined the club he called the captain and the coach 'Sir' and though he grew out of that he was never less then polite and considerate, and never gave less than 100 per cent.

Bleddyn, small and slight, was a fly half. Eric Bann, big and (sometimes) bearded, was a lock and if you described him as irresponsible you were probably being kind to him. Completely erratic where training was concerned he once failed to appear for a first-team game at Northampton and never let a soul know. A lot of captains, me included, tried to get Eric to knuckle down to team discipline and always failed, which did not prevent the next in line swearing to 'get Eric sorted out'. Just when you thought you had he would let you down but no matter how angry you became with him everything was forgotten the next day because he was such superb company. He was the best line-out jumper the club had during my time and any degree of discipline would surely have brought him a cap. He was the complete opposite to John Allen, who never seems to have changed as player or administrator. Quietly effective at scrum half, as treasurer or secretary, to play with him as a hooker was to be in an armchair. John Finlan, in his playing days as an England fly half, described John Allen as the best scrum half he had played with in an England trial.

I always got on well with Garry Adey, who won two England caps as a number eight. Certain aspects of his game were better than anyone else's in the country – his commitment, his tidying of the ball at scrum or line-out, his falling on the ball, the strength in the upper body he exhibited at rucks and mauls. He was unfortunate to play at a time when national selectors were looking for exceptional height in his position, and he always had to give two or three inches to Andy Ripley, Mervyn Davies, Jean-Pierre Bastiat. Nor was he the best ball player in the world, but if you were seeking a balanced back row, there would have been a place for him. It would have been possible for England to have played Garry at number eight and Ripley on a flank but at Leicester Garry played much of his rugby with David Forfar, who, though no great height himself, won a lot of line-out ball through sheer determination. He almost climbed up people and he always responded when Chalkie roared at him during training, or during a game. Chalkie got more out of Dave than anyone could have imagined, just by keeping on his back the whole time. Dave played most of his first-class rugby as a flanker but he came to the club from Syston as a lock. He nearly had his career terminated very early on by an angry Bob Rowell when he kept on knocking Bob out of line-outs during training in an effort to impress.

I first saw Paul Dodge play when he was fifteen, in the youth team on the recreation ground across the road from the main ground. I noticed him first because he seemed bigger than most of the other lads, and then I started to notice his ability. I have never regarded him as anything but special since then. He contributes more to a game than any other centre I have seen and he helps other players enormously. You have only to talk to those who have played with him to see what a high regard they have for him, though he is not always appreciated by onlookers. He is said to be cumbersome, to kick too much; his own view is that he does what seems, in his eyes, to be best for the team and you have only to remember what happened in South Africa in 1980 to evaluate his worth. For some obscure reason he was omitted from the original Lions party; he joined us midway through the tour at Johannesburg as a replacement for the Welsh centre, David Richards, and after he had trained for five minutes everyone knew he would be in the team for the next international. He is all class – his running, his passing, his timing – and no one knows that better than Clive Woodward, whom he has partnered for club and country. Clive knew exactly what he wanted when he came to Leicester from Loughborough University in 1979. Possessed of immense skill, he was as ambitious in his rugby as he is in life itself, but a player of his kind needs a Dodge alongside him. Those two had the best brought out of them by Les Cusworth, who joined from Moseley in 1978. As a fly half he is neither the best tackler nor the best kicker in the country but he brings so much out of other players by his use of the ball, as a runner or distributor. No opposition can ignore him and he has developed so well over the last three years that he became the player Leicester could probably least afford to lose. England, in 1983, knew better.

If I seem to make everything in Leicester's garden seem rosy, it is not of course. Life for a rugby club, for any amateur organization, is seldom that. There are bound to be hiccoughs in the future. For all that the club is well-founded after the success of the last few years, the cost of the upkeep of such a ground as Leicester's is enormous and the club will have to bear in mind the requirements of the Safety of Sports Grounds Act. We have not skimped on resources in maintaining the ground to a high standard, nor on facilities for the youth team which currently contains more potential first-team players than at any other time. The committee structure has improved considerably. But, as with everything else in life, you cannot afford to become complacent, for if you do things will begin to deteriorate. To make sure that standards are maintained, the groundwork must be constantly maintained, or improved. We have now developed a good working relationship with schools and clubs which will continue only if we work at it.

5

Earning My Stripes

Every player who ever reached international standard worked exceptionally hard to get there, but of course some element of luck along the way can help. It helped me, in only my second senior season, when I came from a long way back to take a place in the England party which toured the Far East in September 1971. In my case, however, it would be possible to say I had made my own luck, though John Elliott might not regard it in quite the same light. At the start of the 1970–71 season I was second-choice hooker at Leicester, behind John, waiting for my chance in the first X V whenever he was away or injured. Shortly before Christmas, when we were preparing for the annual game with the Barbarians, he was injured and I had a hand – well, a foot – in it.

The Leicester team had been picked to play the Barbarians, with John in his usual position, and we were training in pairs on the recreation ground, performing a warm-up exercise in which the object was to sweep away your opponent's legs with your own leg. It was entirely an accident – honestly – when I caught John on the ankle. A couple of days later the injury forced him to drop out of the holiday game, leaving me to fill the vacancy. It was John Allen who rang me up in London, where I was spending Christmas with the family, to tell me I was playing in my first big game, a game which not only enabled a lot more people in Leicester to see me playing but also many outsiders, among them the odd selector or two and the national press. My opposite number was David Barry, the Oxford University and

Ireland trials hooker, and Barry John – the year before his coronation in New Zealand – was at fly half in a Baa-baas side which won 18–6. It was a marvellous experience to play before such a huge crowd against so many well-known players and I even recall getting near enough to Barry to tackle him. It must have been anger that lent wings to my feet – I had just lost a ball against the head and the Baa-baas scrum half must have dallied with the ball long enough to allow me to slip out of the scrum and lay a vengeful finger on their star Welshman.

The season had been promising well before Christmas anyway. I had decided to change my county allegiance from Kent to Leicestershire because of all the travelling involved and the fact that whereas Kent played their games on a Wednesday afternoon, which meant having to take a day off work, Leicestershire played on Wednesday evenings. I did so with regret because Kent had treated me well but they were very understanding. Leicestershire invited me to play in their golden jubilee game against Durham, a match in which I scored two tries. I had never consciously worked on my handling or speed at that stage, though it may have been that which got me noticed by many people. I always enjoyed playing sevens, with the old boys and at Leicester, and the games of touch rugby before training were good times for a hooker to test his dummy and sidestep! Perhaps I have been lucky to have something of a feel for ball games, to enjoy running, passing, kicking as much as anyone else, even though my position on a rugby field did not offer too many opportunities.

Leicestershire were happy with my form and picked me for their county championship games in a season when things went well. We reached a play-off for the Midland group title and lost, only 19–16, against a Warwickshire side who had all the stars, England players like David Duckham and Keith Fairbrother, the goal-kicking scrum half, George Cole. It was my games with the county which must have attracted the attention of the national selectors in the first place, for my first-team appearances with Leicester were strictly rationed. At all events, I found myself named as a replacement in England's under-25 match against the touring Fijians at Twickenham in November. I was delighted that someone had even considered me worth a place in an England side, at whatever level, and just as pleased that a club colleague, Garry Adey, was playing in the side. We travelled down to London together on the train with Garry trying to pretend that he really did not have influenza. It was his first big game and he had no wish to drop out, whereas I could just sit back and revel in the big-match atmosphere, along with a cocky scrum half from Wilmslow, Steve Smith, who was on the bench too. It was a foul day and an appalling match which England won 15–11. Garry failed to do himself justice and he was the only member of the team not to go forward to the trial. Six members of that young England side went on to play against Wales at Cardiff, where they were hammered 22–6. They were all new caps and they were joined by a seventh, Charlie Hannaford. Cardiff, of course, has always been the best place for introducing half a new team!

When the Barbarians game fell into my lap, on top of county selection and a nod of recognition from England, it seemed as though someone was waving a magic wand over my season, though, knowing what I know now, it all came too quickly and too easily. It may have been the right time for me to be pressing for a senior place at the club but I had nowhere near served a long enough apprenticeship for high honours. I may have been fortunate that I was beginning my career when a lot of very good club hookers – Andy Johnson from Northampton was one – were nearing the end of their careers and England were looking for promising young men to take the place of deputy to John Pullin, but I did not stop to consider that hookers are seldom ready for the international scene before their mid-twenties. Moreover the role of the hooker was changing. They were beginning to take over the responsibility of throwing in at line-outs and they were required to have a much greater degree of mobility. Players like John Gray, from Loughborough Colleges and Coventry, and myself were among the first of the new breed.

But the season had not finished with me yet. The county championship spilled over into the new year and I became established as Leicester's first-team hooker because the injury to John Elliott took several weeks to clear up. It never gave him much of a chance to reclaim his place and at the end of that season he moved to Nottingham. There was one more big game to come at Leicester, however, that between an oddity of a team labelled Midlands, London and the Home Counties against the Rugby Union President's XV. The president, Bill Ramsay, had invited players from the world's leading rugby countries to play four matches as a contribution towards England's centenary celebrations and it was a quite outstanding party. Since then teams described as a 'world XV' have become comparatively common but this was one of the first and, by general consent, it included all the outstanding players you could think of. Colin Meads, the New Zealand lock who led his country against the 1971 Lions, was there; those two outstanding South Africans, Frik du Preez and Dawie de Villiers, and a host of great names. It was an experience just to watch a giant of a man like Brian Lochore, clad in the eye-catching blue and black quarterings the world team wore, stride out under the lights of Welford Road and survey the scene. It was a bit like being an ordinary man-at-arms watching Sir Lancelot pass by on his way to the next tournament. Their game at Leicester was the first of the four so a lot of attention was focused on it and I regarded myself as lucky even to be a replacement. Lucky is not the word because Andy Johnson, the nominated hooker and England reserve that season, cried off and once more I found myself called upon on the eve of a big game.

It would be too much to have expected to win as well, but we came close enough to it. We lost 18–13 on a day

58

when Bob Hiller, the Harlequins fullback, missed more kicks than he landed, which was most unusual. Du Preez scored two tries, one straight from a kick-off when he ran from halfway through most of the home side at a speed you would never have expected of such a big man. Things went well for me during the game. I had those two experienced Coventry props, Keith Fairbrother and Jim Broderick, on either side of me and Peter Larter and Nigel Horton beavering away just behind. I was quite surprised at the illegal methods used by the Australian hooker, Peter Johnson, to win the ball in the scrum, even allowing for differences in interpretation of the laws down under. It was how I imagine a rugby league hooker performs but I was happy that we held our own, just a few weeks before England announced their party to tour in Japan, Hong Kong and Ceylon. The tour was to take place at the start of the 1971–72 season and, with John Pullin being required by the Lions in New Zealand, and several other senior players being involved in the same tour, there were places going for young men with a disposition to travel – even if this particular young man had never travelled further west than Torquay, or further east than Dover. Maybe it was my appearance that clinched my selection for the party, along with John Gray, because it was in that same season I lost three of my front teeth. Well, you have to take the rough with the smooth. It had happened in a midweek game against Nuneaton, in a quite innocuous incident, when I ran round the front of a line-out and caught the Nuneaton scrum half's elbow in my mouth as his arm came swinging back after he had delivered his pass. The teeth were cracked and out they had to come. I lost a fourth six years later, with the Lions in New Zealand.

Even that, it seemed, failed to spoil my luck completely because three days later we played Llanelli at Welford Road and won 12–3. I was sitting in the clubhouse after the game feeling pleased with myself because I had scored a few points – I was goal-kicker too in those days, the result of winning an early-season competition in training when we had no established kicker. But I had almost acknowledged the fact that a bloke with no front teeth and no false teeth to fill the yawning gap was unlikely to meet with much success at the players' dance later that evening. It was, I reckoned, a night for a few jars when in walked an attractive blonde looking for one of our flankers, Chris Baynes. She was the bearer of a message from her brother and lingered for a moment before leaving a telephone number where Chris could contact her. After she left my resolutions regarding the effect of my empty gums on some young girl wavered – we blond(e)s must stick together – and I called the number and invited her to the dance. To my surprise she accepted. This was Margaret Crossley, daughter of a Yorkshireman from Brighouse but brought up in Tees-side. She was at Leicester University studying for an education degree. Not only can she teach, she sings, plays the piano and guitar, retains an active interest in hockey and tennis, and is now doing time bringing up two young Wheelers after eleven years of marriage. As I said, that was a good season.

It did not matter, either, that England went east very much in the shadow of the Lions and their outstanding achievements against the All Blacks. The Far East tour party was selected with an eye on the future and perhaps today I would not agree with all their selections, including as it did so many newcomers. The same mistake was made in Australia four years later, with dire results. The party, which was managed by Bob Weighill (who became secretary to the Rugby Union two years later) and coached by John Burgess was: Jim Broderick, Fran Cotton, Dick Cowman, David Robinson, John Finlan, Peter Glover, John Gray, Charlie Hannaford, Jeremy Janion, Peter Larter, Bob Lloyd, Tony Neary, Chris Ralston, Budge Rogers (captain), Peter Rossborough, Dave Roughley, Nigel Starmer-Smith, Mike Hannell, Roger Uttley, Chris Wardlow, Rod Webb, Jan Webster and me. Geoff Evans, the Coventry centre, joined us later as a replacement for Roughley.

I began the tour with the impression that I would be second-choice hooker. Perhaps I had a bit of an inferiority complex about my own ability then, even though I had played in the last big game of the 1970–71 season, or perhaps it was a healthy respect for Gray's ability. I have a photograph taken on that tour of John and me and, in terms of physique, it has all the quality of 'man against boy'. He was a tremendous player and it was a good day for me when I heard he had signed professional forms to play rugby league. I knew that if he and I were to spend our playing time as rivals it would not always work out in my favour, as it seemed to do in those early days. His subsequent success in the league game only bears out my high opinion of him; as a hooker pure and simple he had technical deficiencies but he was a great all-round forward, very strong and very tough. However, I was chosen for the first game against Waseda University, during which I kicked three conversions including one from touch in pouring rain – I cannot remember what fate had overcome our regular kicker that day – and I played again in the next game, against All Japan, which we won 27–19. Then I caught tonsillitis and did not even see the next game, against All Japan, which was won 6–3.

Several players came together on that tour who served England well during the seventies. Cotton, Neary and Ralston had already played for England the previous season. Uttley had to wait another two years, and I waited another four. In many ways it was an experimental tour; none of the home countries had been to the Far East and the conditions were new to most of us. We were missing several first-choice players and we had a coach who was hoping to do well and press his claims for the England post. I was impressed with Burgess, by his obvious sincerity, his organization and attention to detail. He even managed to produce a tour songbook with the lyrics to forty songs, old and not so old. Some of his ideas were quite revolutionary to many of us (some turned out to be impractical) but he was desperately keen to succeed. I had the impression that he did not have the greatest rapport with the manager, which may have been reflected by the announcement, ten days after the tour ended, that John Elders was to coach England. It was possibly an undeserved rebuff for Burgess; the players felt they had done reasonably well, even if some of the journalists who joined the tour after accompanying the Lions round New Zealand were not entirely impressed. We won all our games in unfamiliar surroundings, frequently on sub-standard pitches, frequently in intense heat, with a very mixed bag of players.

For me it was a taste of what was to come but, after our return to England, I had to go back to school, as it were, and learn my trade properly. I caught some form of malaria on tour which affected me for several months. Often in the night I would wake up in a cold sweat and my form suffered. I was picked for the Midlands in the regional trial and, knowing John Gray was on the bench, I was reluctant to cry off but I was not playing well and it showed. I disappeared from the national rankings and the Metropolitan policeman, Tony Boddy, came in as deputy hooker to Pullin that season. It was no bad thing, I was only twenty-two and I had not even played a full season as my club's senior hooker. There was so much to learn and, in any case, things had happened so quickly that I had hardly developed the ambition to play for my country in the international championship. I was still young enough to be pleased and surprised in accepting any honours which came my way. One journalist I spoke to that season told me not to worry, that I would go with England to South Africa in 1972 and my career would develop from there, but it did not. John White, Pullin's deputy at Bristol, became his England deputy too and went with England on their 1973 tour to New Zealand, a tour for which I had no pretensions. I was still learning, I had also been elected club captain – I had enough on my plate. It was nice to hear, though, that between the time England cancelled their scheduled visit to Argentina (because of an outbreak of guerilla warfare) and replaced

62

it with the visit to New Zealand, John Gray turned professional. That was one rival out of the way.

As it turned out, I had not been entirely forgotten. The non-travelling reserve cards continued to drop through the door of the rented cottage in Newtown Linford, which was our first home after Margaret and I were married. Before I grappled with the intricacies of club captaincy there were triumphs of a more domestic nature to enjoy: the quality of rugby played by Leicester under the leadership of Graham Willars which brought us 988 points one season; the addition to the strength of Alan Old, the Middlesbrough and England fly half; of a Welsh flank forward from Madeley College who was to gain a certain notoriety several years later, Paul Ringer. I also received a hint of the nature of New Zealand rugby at its best, when Ian Kirkpatrick's All Blacks played Midland Counties (East) at Welford Road in January 1973. It was one of the few occasions on a largely unhappy tour when the All Blacks let their hair down and the Midland side, with eight Leicester players, was trounced 43–12.

The next season, however, I was restored to England's fold; the Australians were here on a short tour and though it was the Bristol pair of Pullin and White who had been England's hookers in New Zealand a few months previously, I was reserve to Pullin for the international against Australia – which was the first time I had ever watched a full international at Twickenham – and remained so for the 1974 championship season. It was a good way to be re-introduced to top-class rugby and at last I began to wake up to the fact that, if I worked hard enough, I could be England's hooker. I was beginning to dream of the day when the number two jersey would be mine – Pullin was thirty-two and could not go on for ever, fine player though he was. I wanted to take a full part at an international weekend, not merely that of a spare. I have no doubt that substitutes involved with representative teams which I have captained have criticized me for not ensuring that they felt part of the overall build-up but I have been in their position and I

63

know that, if you are not actually chosen for the game, you are out on a limb. A player with no role to play.

I did find a positive role in the annual Mobbs Memorial match at Northampton that year though. Leicester had not had one of their 'own' players – by which I mean a player who established himself through the lower teams as opposed to a passing star like Arneil or Old – chosen for the Barbarians for some seasons but I was invited to play against the East Midlands that year and set up a record for a hooker by scoring three of the eight Barbarian tries. It was one of those matches in which everything fell into my lap – I did not even have to demonstrate my devastating sidestep, in fact I don't think I ran much more than 10 yards for any of the tries. Not surprisingly, I had not scored three tries in a match before, nor have I since, though I did manage to accumulate over 500 points during thirteen years with Leicester (156 of them in the 1974–75 season when I was the club's leading points scorer). That Barbarians match, conceivably, may have helped me towards a reserve card for the 1974 Lions tour to South Africa, a year when another England hooker, Pullin, was overlooked both as captain and tourist. As in 1983, Ireland wound up top of the championship pile and England were at the bottom – and they say lightning doesn't strike twice.

It was that same year that England played two games against France, the second a charity international to raise funds for relatives after the horrifying aeroplane crash on 3 March when many supporters returning from England's game in Paris were killed. I had some hopes of playing in that game but, as England lost heavily, it may have been a good one to miss and by the time the 1974–75 season came along it seemed as though the selectors were ready to discard their long-serving Bristol hooker. The Barbarians asked me to be replacement to Bobby Windsor for their game in November against New Zealand and the following month, despite the defeat of the Midlands by the North in a regional trial at Leeds,

England picked me in the senior side in the final trial. Not that they were going to do me too many favours: I was in there with Cotton and Colin White against the old Gloucestershire firm, Burton, Pullin and Cowling. The fact that Robin Cowling had joined Leicester that season from Gloucester did not mean any lessening of effort on his part because, like myself, he was conscious of being nearer than ever before to an England cap, only he had fewer years in which to achieve it. Having been a replacement several times I was trying desperately hard to succeed but it was a strain suddenly to find myself regarded as the senior hooker. In a trial situation it is very frequently best to be on the junior side, especially if you are a forward, because you can be as disruptive as you like. The senior side is instructed to develop as much teamwork as possible in the hope that the whole side will play well and can then go through to the first international en bloc. I was defending a situation, that of England hooker, that I had not even won yet, against a man who had the better part of forty caps behind him and one of the best tight-head props at winning ball in the country. Although we won, the 'England' front row lost a few balls against the head; it was Pullin who played against Ireland while Cowling and I held hands on the replacements bench and wondered if it would ever be our turn.

I did manage to play some significant part in the build-up to the match though. By this time John Burgess had succeeded Elders as England coach; he introduced us to regional squad weekends, to such esoteric developments as echelon running, to complex penalty routines which needed two or three years to master rather than the two or three months which were available to us. The players did their best to adjust to the way Burgess wanted to play, appreciating his blunt Lancastrian sincerity, his willingness to give everything to the cause of England rugby. In the dressing room at Lansdowne Road I had my first chance to listen to his fire-and-brimstone pre-match talk; the intensity of the occasion was immense and the climax of his talk came when he grabbed an England shirt, pointed to the red rose and told us, bursting with emotion: 'When you get tired and there's still ten minutes to go, take a look at this rose and ask yourself what it means to you.' The shirt he grabbed was mine, with me in it, and I was yanked out of my corner and almost brandished bodily at the rest of the squad. We went out and England lost 12–9, a defensive muddle when time was running out allowing Billy McCombe, the Irish fly half, in for the decisive try. Still, we had come close to beating the champions on their own ground and it seemed no time to make changes; had we kicked one more penalty everyone would have been happy but defeat meant that the selectors felt obliged to do something. Back in the team's hotel, just an hour and a half after the match, Burgess called us together in his room for one of his 'honesty' sessions. 'Let's be honest with each other,' he would say, 'let's try and sort out what went wrong.' Obviously you try and pinpoint the reasons for defeat and eradicate them, but not just after the game when the players are physically and mentally drained. The next day, or the next squad session but not with your hair still wet from the bath. No player wants to analyse what went wrong that quickly; nor does he wish to receive an invitation to point the finger at any one department of the side and blame them for defeat as I felt we were being asked to do.

The following week we had a squad session at Coventry, when the team to play France in the next game was to be announced. 'For the first time in a long while we've decided to leave John out of the team,' Burgess told us. 'John, John, there aren't too many Johns in the squad,' I thought before it clicked that it was Pullin he was referring to and I was in for my first cap. I skipped out onto the Coundon Road pitch like a spring lamb – not a common experience for a Leicester player, considering the rivalry between us and Coventry. Pullin had been told beforehand that he was to be dropped, which must have helped slightly – it has not always been the case. He wished me luck but he was even kinder when he rang me at work the next day. 'Someone calling himself John Pullin on the line,' a colleague told me. 'Pull the other one,' I said, reflecting that though I had received many calls congratulating me that day, John was hardly likely to be among them. But it was Pullin, offering me some extra match tickets because he knew that as many family and relations as possible would want to go to Twickenham for my first international. That showed a lot of thought at a time when he must have been feeling a bit low.

My selection received a mixed press, one commentator suggesting that one reason for my playing was because I added to the goal-kicking strength! The nearest I got to it was to act as placer for the kicker on a day when the wind was too strong to leave the ball standing by itself. I was not the only change. Martin Cooper replaced Old at fly half, Roger Uttley and John Watkins came in at lock and flanker for Billy Beaumont and Peter Dixon. There was no need for four changes from the team against Ireland but that, in those days, is how selection went. I was the only new cap though the French had three, including Cholley, the tight-head prop, and the twenty-two-year-old flanker, Jean-Pierre Rives. Propping me were Cotton, who was captain, and the Cornish loose-head, Stack Stevens, who was thirty-three and in his last international season. It was not a good match, from England's point of view. We lost 27–20, scoring two tries to four by France, and we ended looking something of a shambles because, with time running out and some leeway to make up, we began to try some of Burgess's tapped penalty moves in the hope that we would catch the French napping. It was completely the wrong time to do so: even if we had been winning and the confidence had been running high we had not had sufficient time in which to rehearse them. As it was the timing and passing was poor and half of us did not know where we were supposed to be running anyway.

But even the result could not spoil the day entirely . . .

the sense of occasion was tremendous even if half the morning was spent in nerve-ridden trips to the hotel loo. The coach drive to the ground, the vast crowd and all of them, it seems, looking at you, wondering – just as you are yourself – whether the man will match up to the moment. I could not tell you anything about the game itself, except that I was penalized once for foot-up. Playing international rugby for the first time is entirely a matter of reacting to what is happening around you – there is no time to think ahead and it always takes two or three games before you adjust to the pace and suddenly find yourself in a position to plan for more than just the fleeting moment. But I was desperate for someone to give me their opinion of my game. I had no yardstick by which I could make any judgement for myself and sat after the game, hoping that someone, anyone, would give me a reaction, even if it was only to say I was rubbish. It was Tony Neary who came up with the necessary reassurance. 'Well done,' he said, and that was all I needed. Even though there were four changes in the side to play Wales at Cardiff, I was reselected which took a great weight off my mind. No one wants to be written off as a one-cap wonder.

If I had been in any doubt about it after the French game, the Cardiff encounter confirmed my feeling that the major difference between club and international rugby is the pressure on the scrummage. It is true that there is a noticeable difference in the pace of the game but, for a forward, the set-piece pressure is enormous. We faced the redoubtable Pontypool front row that day and Graham Price, Bobby Windsor and Charlie Faulkner had Allan Martin and another scrummaging lock, Geoff Wheel, right behind them. It added up to an outstanding Welsh pack and the pressure told on Stack who was playing loose-head. Price had split him away from me so I was acting as the base through which the England second row were transmitting their shove. At the same time I was still trying to hook the ball. Something had to give under the immense pressure and,

68

in the end, it was me. At a scrum just on half-time Cotton went up on the tight-head side, the Welsh drive came through, and, as my chin went down on my chest, I heard something crack in my neck. Immediately that area began to stiffen so off I went, leaving Pullin to come on as replacement. There was no specialist in neck injuries available at the ground and no one wanted to miss the second half of the game so I was dispatched to Cardiff Royal Infirmary to join the queue of Saturday afternoon casualties, children who had fallen out of trees, damaged motor cyclists and the like. Eventually I was X-rayed, given some pills and told to see a specialist in Leicester on the Monday.

It was the first and, happily, the last time I was seriously injured playing rugby, although a neck injury must always be the main fear of a front-row forward, if he pauses long enough to think about it. If you spend all your life reflecting upon what might happen, of course, you never leave the safety of your living room. When the damage was properly assessed it was discovered that I had broken a bone in the vertebra which had been knocked slightly out of line by the continual scrummage pressure. X-rays showed the piece of broken bone floating around and initial reaction was unfavourable – the Rugby Union's doctor, Leo Walkden, advised me in the first instance to take up golf though at that stage few tests had been carried out.

Medical opinion came to accept the fact that, if there was any way I could play again, I would. A series of exhaustive checks were made until finally my consultant at the Leicester Royal Infirmary, who had played rugby himself and was aware of the intense motivation within individual players, gave me the go-ahead to continue my career. I was advised not to play if I could feel any pain in the neck, which might indicate that the injury was in an unstable condition, but, as I understand it, by now the broken bone has calcified and created three rigid vertebrae. If I ever have the misfortune to break my neck, the damage will, I imagine, be spectacular.

It is quite understandable that the doctors should have been cautious about expressing an opinion that I could play again. Neck injuries cannot be taken lightly, particularly if you intend to subject the neck to the unnatural amount of strain that scrummaging imposes. But it is comforting to know that the school of thought which divides sporting injuries from other injuries is expanding because apart, from anything else, it takes into account the different mental approach and high degree of basic fitness of injured players. People like John (J.P.R.) Williams and his wife, Scilla, by setting up special clinics for the treatment of sporting injuries, are having a two-way effect: they increase the awareness of rugby clubs of the need for better medical facilities and they may help to demonstrate to the medical profession itself that sporting injuries should be regarded in a new light. It is not so long ago when, for many clubs, medical facilities were limited to a sponge, elastoplast and, for serious cases, a packet of Players No. 6! That situation has improved greatly over the last ten years. At Leicester we have been very fortunate to have struck up an exceptional relationship with the Leicester Royal Infirmary, which is, literally, just across the road from the ground. We have a decently equipped medical room at the ground and enthusiastic doctors among the members who are glad to help all they can. We have a physiotherapist in attendance at training nights for those players who need attention and an arrangement with the Infirmary so that players needing treatment after a game can come in on Sunday mornings. Some clubs may have better arrangements; many obviously will not because money is usually short, rugby clubs being amateur organizations, and medical facilities are, inevitably, costly.

But at least the need for good medical arrangements is generally recognized now, not least among major touring parties who are accompanied by their own doctor and physiotherapist. That facility is quite invaluable and the physio tends to become the most overworked member of any touring party. His hotel room becomes regarded as the players' meeting place at any hour of the day or night because there will always be someone wanting treatment and always someone looking for a chat. Don Gatherer – 'Snake' as he has become known to the players – is now the most put-upon member of England parties but, thanks to his skill as a physio, injuries which might otherwise have taken weeks to heal have improved rapidly within days.

A serious injury, of whatever kind, does have the effect of concentrating the mind upon the possible long-term consequences of playing a physical game like rugby and who it is that should take the decision as to whether a player resumes or not. During this last season considerable publicity has been given to injured rugby players, particularly to youngsters, but I believe it is fair to say that, given the large numbers of people playing the game, serious damage happens very rarely. Apart from this incident in 1975 I have suffered only the usual run of niggling sprains, bumps and bruises which any sportsman or woman can expect. The worst injury I have seen while playing was that suffered by the Leicester wing, Tim Barnwell, in the 1983 John Player final, when a clash of heads in a tackle induced a blood clot on the brain which required an emergency operation. But no one could have legislated for that, it was pure accident, just as was Maurice Colclough's knee injury in 1983, when he fell awkwardly after tripping over Colin Smart's leg. You have to define what a 'serious' injury is. Many people, young and old, break a limb at one time or another without going anywhere near a rugby field. A cut that requires stitching may seem nasty but it mends after a few weeks, and while I am not suggesting that one should expect to be stitched up after every game, everyone who plays rugby must accept the element of risk in a game which necessitates physical confrontation. What remains quite unacceptable is the player who sets out to put an opponent off the field by deliberately injuring him. That such players do exist is regrettably

71

true; they are known to other players, and they should be known to club committees who are in the best possible position to prevent them from playing the game.

Equally club officials must accept some responsibility when it comes to choosing players who have been ill or injured, though the major responsibility must lie with the player himself. Players do not always take a mature attitude. In their anxiety to regain a team place, at whatever level, they often convince themselves that they are fit. It will soon become apparent that they are not, and hence the need for the fitness test which, if passed successfully, will give both player and selectors confidence. Whenever a player has to take time away from the game because of injury, there must always be some lurking doubt about fitness when he returns. A rigorous test will remove that doubt. The player, therefore, must be at some pains not to conceal anything, however great his desire to get back in the side. Selectors too must avoid the feeling that the restoration of one player who has been injured, however good his general form, will 'make' their team. Very few individual players make such a difference to a team, but if one player is regarded in that light it is only because of his contribution when he is 100 per cent fit. If he is only operating at 95 per cent fitness, that will not be good enough, and he will suddenly be seen as an ordinary, rather than an exceptional, player. His presence in a team will then have the opposite effect from that intended; his colleagues will quickly realize if he is still carrying an injury; his opponents will see that there is less to fear from him than they thought. I played a county game shortly after a bout of flu because I was reluctant to see someone else take the spot I had worked hard for, but I knew as soon as I ran onto the field that I should not have been there. By then, it is too late. I learned my lesson. The higher up the representative ladder you go, the more difficult it becomes to take the decision about declaring unfitness. You take note of your own medical adviser's feelings and of the stage the season has reached; if, for instance, you are picked for the last international of the season and you have an injury which, with the help of a pain-killing injection, will not affect your game, should you then declare yourself fit? If there is the possibility of permanent physical damage it is not worth the risk. If, on the other hand, it merely means that the injury will take another three weeks to clear up, rather than just one week, then I believe that is acceptable. You must remember that the desire among all internationals to continue playing the game at the highest level is quite exceptional. The Rugby Union's policy is that if a player needs a pain-killer, he is not fit, which, broadly speaking, I would agree with, but I would still maintain that there are circumstances in which an injection can be justified.

All of which takes us a long way from the Cardiff National Stadium on 15 February 1975. With only a fortnight between the game with Wales and the Calcutta Cup match it was impossible that I should be fit to play against Scotland but I was keen to notify John Burgess that the doctors said I would be available for selection for the England tour to Australia during the summer. The party was to be chosen immediately after the Calcutta Cup game, which England won 7–6. By the time I knew I would be fit to tour it was the day of the game and I could not contact Burgess until the team had returned to the Hilton Hotel after the game. Understandably as coach he was euphoric after having seen England win for the first time and he may not have taken in everything I was trying to say. In the event I was left out, apparently on medical grounds. It was felt, understandably perhaps from a selectorial point of view, that my neck injury might be exacerbated on the hard grounds in Australia. Pullin remained number one choice and Jon Raphael, who was then playing for Bective Rangers in Ireland, went as number two.

It was a disappointment but, unlike 1971, I knew that all the groundwork had been done and that I could challenge for the spot the following season from a firm basis. I was lucky too to have an alternative to fall back on. Ian Robertson, who was approaching the end of his own playing career, had invited me to join the Public School Wanderers visit to Zimbabwe and South Africa if England did not require my services. So while England found themselves embattled down under, on the losing end in both internationals, I was in the company of some very fine players, who turned out some excellent rugby. Innocent as I still was in policy matters, it nevertheless struck me as odd that a flanker as good as John Watkins was with me in Zimbabwe; I assumed that Steve Callum must be a quite outstanding prospect, even though he played for Upper Clapton. It may be that Burgess, imbued as he was with new ideas, was looking for younger players whom he could mould to his ways; it may be that England, having beaten South Africa and New Zealand on tour in 1972 and 1973, and having seen off a disappointing Australian side in England in 1973, felt that a tour to Australia was a softer option and that they could experiment. All four home countries and, indeed, New Zealand, have found over the last decade that a tour of Australia is hardly soft, which is why they have been awarded a Lions tour of their own in 1989.

In the meantime I learned from experienced players like Fergus Slattery of Ireland and his fellow countrymen in the PSW front row, Ned Byrne and Paddy Agnew. It was a great tour, the sun shone, we were superbly looked after. We enjoyed each other's company, we played well and so, if it is possible not to miss touring with one's national side, I did not miss being trampled underfoot by some highly motivated Australians. There was, I suppose, a degree of danger that Raphael could slip ahead of me in the ratings but I was much more confident, having played for England. I knew that I could compete at that level, that I could take the jump in playing standard in my stride. A final reflection on my first season as an international: the step between club and country seems greater in rugby than in other sports, though I have not been able to make up my mind why. Perhaps it is the crowds, so much greater for internationals than at club games, perhaps it is the scrutiny of the television and the ballyhoo in the press. Football players take big crowds and press coverage for granted. Perhaps, also, when you have as many as fifteen players in a side, there has to be a bigger overall increase in ability. Whatever the difference, though, I knew I could bridge it.

6

Leader of the Pack

As a rugby player you give of your best and hope for promotion, whether the next step up is the school second XV, Leicester's first team, or England or the Lions. If you are then awarded the captaincy that is obviously a bonus but it is also an extra responsibility which increases the higher the level at which you operate.

I would love to captain England in a full international. After all, Tonga away is not quite the same as Wales at Twickenham. There was some possibility of leading England in 1977 but it was only a vague possibility and, when Billy Beaumont was given the job, I put it out of my mind. After all, Billy was three years younger than me so his career was always going to outlast mine. But a head injury in February 1982, the culmination of a series of bumps on the head that a player like him was always likely to sustain, forced Billy's premature retirement. That was the time when, if the captaincy had been offered me, I was ready for it and there was no vastly experienced alternative to hand. I had had a second spell of club captaincy, making five seasons in all, I had experienced two Lions tours and I had played another twenty games for England.

Even then it was not a clearcut situation. Billy, we thought, would only miss the game against Ireland and so Steve Smith was appointed 'caretaker' for a game we lost by one point. My own fitness at the time meant there was a doubt whether I would play. Before the next game, however, Billy was forced to retire which opened up a completely new vista. I thought that because both Steve and I were in similar positions – age was creeping up on us – the selectors might look to the future and make John Scott captain. But Steve retained the captaincy and though he went on to do as good a job as anybody could have done, I knew that only exceptional circumstances would ever allow me another chance of leading my country. Only the selectors know why they chose as they did. I felt that there may have been some antipathy towards Leicester because we tended to take an independent view of matters dear to the Rugby Union's heart. I have also heard that Budge Roger's the chairman, regarded me as akin to a 'professional' because of my contact with the Adidas company, a relationship which I shall discuss later. Whatever the reason, I came to feel that captain of England was one honour that would pass me by.

Captaincy imposes different demands on you, depending on whether you are leading a club or a representative side, and depending upon whether that side is successful or not. My own first experience of captaincy came in 1973 and it was not a situation of my own choosing. Leicester had elected a popular centre, Mike Yandle, as captain but his firm moved him to Wales and it was suggested that I ought to stand as his replacement. I had not completed three seasons as the club's first-team hooker at that stage; I was only twenty-four and I did not believe I was ready for it.

I was lucky in that my first season was reasonably successful and that I had Chalkie White, the club coach, to help me express myself. But one of the lessons I learned very quickly is that you must be yourself as captain: if you are not a table-thumper by nature then it is no use trying to be one. If your way is to be quiet and persuasive, that is the way to do it. The players will see through anything that's false straight away; any kind of act will have the opposite effect to the one you want. In my first year as Leicester's captain I had this naive idea that if the lads were enjoying themselves they would play well. We had some great away trips as a result but gradually I realized that getting drunk every Saturday night after matches was not the way to a great season, however enjoyable it might be. One of the basic truths of captaincy is that if you get it right on the field of play, which involves a tremendous amount of preparation and forethought, then the good nights will come as a direct consequence.

I did not have the experience, or the knowledge, to be dogmatic about anything and I had to rely considerably on the senior players in the side. What I did have to offer was enthusiasm and commitment, which is still a large part of the captain's game at club level. Many players will take a lead from the captain's attitude but I could have been a lot more forceful in getting my message across instead of just doing what I thought was right and hoping others would follow. A larger problem presented itself the following season, my second term as captain, when the results were poorer and I was away more often at representative matches or squad training. It is incredibly difficult to come to selection on a Monday evening when you have, perhaps, been an international replacement and missed the club's Saturday game, which has been lost. I would go along believing that certain players should be in the team without having the least idea of how they had played two days earlier, and I found the job of captain drifting away from me.

The problem is that whatever the selection committee may decide, the captain is the one who has to tell the player he has been dropped. There is no earthly point telling that player: 'Yes, I wanted you in but they didn't.' You have to give the view of the committee and if you do not believe that view is right, it is almost impossible to tell players – who are very committed to achieving a first-team place – that they have been dropped. In any case, most of them believe they deserve the place and if you tell them someone they think can't play for peanuts has been picked ahead of them, you have to be very sure of your own ground and still be prepared for an ear-bashing.

That, though, is one of the responsibilities of the

captain. If, however, you are sure that changes have been made for the right reasons (and very often with a losing team there is a great temptation to change for the sake of being seen to be doing something about an unacceptable situation) you can face players and explain the decision. You can still be sympathetic to their views. Many selection decisions are very close in any case and, even at the highest level, sometimes you find that if you ask a committee member why such-and-such a change was made, you will find that he is not really sure. It can be explained as being no more than a feeling, an optimistic feeling, that the newcomer may be the answer. But if you drop someone you must know exactly why and, equally, just why his replacement was chosen. It is only fair to both parties.

This is only one example of the sort of situation that can arise at any club and with which the captain has to deal. Let us say you have a back-row forward who misses a tackle and the opposition score a try as a result, which gives them a one-point win. You must remember that, but for a kickable penalty that went wide, you might still have won, and the flanker's missed tackle would have been less significant. Because you lost, however, you may feel you must tighten up in that area, but what sort of a player is the next in line, in the second team, and how will he affect the balance of your whole back row? You must avoid any frivolous selections and that may be difficult when you have such a broad cross-section to select from as we do at Leicester, where the captain and team secretary of the thirds have the same voting power as the captain and coach of the firsts. Once selection has been talked through and you are happy with the arguments, even if you do not wholly agree with them, then you can face the player concerned. There were very few occasions at Leicester in my second spell as captain (between 1978 and 1981) when selection went against what Chalkie and I wanted because we tended to work it out on the telephone so carefully the evening before.

What you do or say on the field itself can come only

with experience. I shudder to think now of some of the decisions I made – or, as importantly, failed to make – in my first two years as captain. Much of the time captaincy during a game depends on taking opportunities as they arise. A chance may come to do or say something and if you miss it it will not come again. And if you are not one who naturally lays down the law, it is very easy to keep quiet, to think what should be done but not say it. I must have missed so many of them in my early days, yet it all came with greater experience. You have to learn somehow. Billy Beaumont learned when he was actually captain of England, having never captained a side since his school days. His experience in the game, however, was greater than mine had been at club level; therefore his learning period was shorter.

The individual games against touring sides or in trial situations need a completely different approach from club captaincy. The club job lasts for nearly ten months of the year, beginning in July, when you start to draw up training schedules, and ending at the start of May. It involves three, and sometimes four, nights a week. You must decide where to train, who will take charge, where the training weekend (if you have one) will take place. A good first-team secretary, as we have at Leicester, will take a lot of the burden of telephoning players, making sure your potential first-team squad know what is happening and emphasizing how important it is that they should all attend. When the season begins the captain has to ensure the attitude of his players is correct and give constant encouragement to his forwards during the game. As a forward captain I was happy to leave my halfbacks free to make their own decisions. That is part of their job; they are the people who control any game and they do not need a captain to tell them what to do. I was fortunate in having some very good players at scrum half and fly half at Leicester. Alan Old was at the club when I began as captain and it would have been fairly pointless my telling such an experienced England fly half what to do. If I had something constructive to say I would say it, otherwise, as a forward, you must confidently assume that your backs will make the right decisions. You may, of course, decide that the play is too wide and that, for five minutes, a short game, played down the blind side and off the back row, is advisable. If you have a young player at halfback you may need to give him plenty of encouragement. But overall, the side that gets it right mentally before and during the game will stand a better chance of winning, no matter how much talent the opposition have. The Barbarians game with Leicester at Christmas time is always a classic example of that, when Leicester generally play at a far higher level than expected; because they are so keyed up for the game they play to what must be, in fact, their genuine potential.

There are instances during a game when, as captain, you can directly influence the outcome. Some decisions regarding penalties can be vital, depending on the stage the game has reached. Should you kick for touch, go for goal, take a tapped penalty? Making the correct decision amounts to having a feel for the game. An example occurred in the 1979 cup final against Moseley; we were 12–9 down when we were awarded a penalty on halfway. Dusty Hare might have kicked it and got three points but we ran it because that was the point when we were beginning to go forward and getting a degree of impetus into their half. We developed confidence from running the ball at Moseley and eventually we won the position for the scrum from which we scored the winning try. The penalty kick at goal, a difficult one, might have missed its target and the touchfinder could have put us back with a line-out on halfway, nothing gained. There are times when you must control your goal-kicker, because some players, not Dusty perhaps, are very ambitious about their kicking and like to grab all the opportunities possible to score points. You have to be realistic about their chances because if the percentages suggest you are not going to score, you would do far better to put the ball down in the corner and create pressure from there.

When you come to the stage of leading a representative side there is a great deal of responsibility, a wider area of people to consider, yet it is so much easier to focus into a specific three-week period of possibly two training sessions and the game itself. You have no selection responsibilities, there is a definite set of circumstances: this is your team, this is your opposition, the game will be played at this place on this day, your object is to win it. You can plan exactly what you are going to say and do as captain during the build-up and I was lucky to have Chalkie White as coach to many of the representative sides I captained. We could dovetail our roles. Both of us developed a feeling for what was required without the need for great debate. Moving up from club to county or district captaincy and thence to national captaincy is always a frightening prospect. Can you cope, can you motivate players you don't know so well, can you say the right things in the team meeting, put yourself across in training, control things on the field? Like everything else, once you have got the first match behind you, it is that much easier.

But you never stop worrying about the team. As a player you have only yourself to worry over. As captain you must worry not only about your own game but that of the other fourteen players. You also have to cope with the team's public image, the questions that come from the press and the public. That was a role I found comparatively easy. It is just question and answer rather than the dredging up of profound thoughts on the game that are required in a team talk to a group of hardened players who have seen it all anyway. When journalists talk about any game in which I have been involved, there are very few areas which I have not already considered deeply. Whatever question is asked, I have almost certainly pondered the answer some time before or, if not, the coach has or someone else has and it is all worked out. I enjoyed the public side and, in general, journalists have been very fair with me. They may try and lead in a particular direction, perhaps to try to get you to agree with their view of any game, but they seldom try to put you on the spot.

On the one occasion I did captain England I was a long way from the madding crowd of press and public. It came at the end of England's Far East tour of 1979. Billy had gone through a couple of games with a painful ear infection and it became sufficiently uncomfortable for him to drop out of the game with Tonga. It was a little difficult to take the game seriously because conditions and facilities were, to put it kindly, primitive compared with what we were used to. A patch of grass near the beach was the training area and the pitch itself, at Nuku 'Alofa, was patches of sand littered with sea shells and one rickety old grandstand. I wanted very much to get things right and sat up late the night before thinking what I might say in my team talk. We left the hotel already changed and made our way to the ground. There was only a little room under the stand where we could put on our boots and do our final warm-up, a room where the groundsman kept his bicycle. It was padlocked and nobody could find a key so one of the locals picked up a rock and knocked the padlock off. In we filed, into this musty dark room with little more than six feet headroom – the groundsman removed his bike. We emerged blinking into the sunlight to be introduced to the King of Tonga, a twenty-four-stone giant, one of whose sons was playing in the game. Despite all these distractions, which made it difficult to keep minds focused on the match, the players maintained discipline in the face of a hard start when the Tongans went off like firecrackers. We won 37–17 which may make me the only undefeated England captain of modern times.

I played for England under a series of great players, most of them great forwards from the north country. That was one of England's problems at the time, until they lit upon Billy. They had Neary, Cotton and Uttley all playing together and the selectors kept trying each of them in turn when things failed to go quite the expected way. None of them got enough time to develop as captains but I had immense respect for them all. I was never conscious of a great tactical awareness among them, possibly because in my position as hooker it is often difficult to judge who has said what that might have affected the course of a game. But you must have respect for the captain as a player; the common denominator among international players is the competitive instinct and the fact that they are all self-motivated. In a club team you will inevitably have some players from whom you have to drag the best but in an international dressing room you know you will not have that problem. All the players know the score and all they are looking for in the captain is someone with a bit of organization to make sure the attitude is right. There is a skill, too, in the captain noticing the one or two players who may, just for once, need a lift if they have come back from a recent injury, which may still be on their minds, or if they have to face a particularly difficult opponent. Players must have confidence in the captain so that they can take their grumbles to him and know they will be heard with sympathy.

Fran Cotton was captain during my first international season, in 1975, and he was everything I needed as a forward. He was forthright, a superbly aggressive prop, his attitude was just right. Take him away from the rugby field and he is an equally great man. He related well to players – all these north countrymen did – and his background with Loughborough Colleges and Lancashire ensured that he knew a great deal about the game. What is a good captain? A man you would follow anywhere and Fran was exactly that. When Fran was buzzing he was hard, positive in his scrummaging, involved in every piece of important play in the most constructive way. It was injury and illness, the legacy of the Lions tour in 1980, that finally ended his career against Wales in 1981.

One of my main memories of Fran as captain comes from the game that the North and Midlands played against Argentina in 1976, a game which no one expected us to win because they had won all their games in Wales and were to go on to defeat against the full Welsh side by just one point. Fran concentrated on the one object, victory, and you have only to talk to some of the non-internationals who played that day, who had little to do with Fran, to realize what an impression he made. David Forfar, the Leicester flanker, would tell anyone he thought the world of Fran. Given more consistency of selection Fran could have captained England for several seasons, not just one.

That same season, 1974–75, the captaincy passed to Tony Neary, the Broughton Park flanker who led England throughout the following season. The fact that England won no games at all in 1975–76 was no reflection on Tony's playing ability. He is a very clever man, great fun off the pitch, and perhaps we had a special rapport because his birthday is the day before mine. I do not consider him the most natural of captains in the way that Roger Uttley, who succeeded him, was. A tremendously honest man, Roger's major asset was that he could talk so well to players, and not in a superficial manner. During the build-up to any international there are long periods of time to be filled in, periods of waiting for something to happen which can get on anyone's nerves. Nothing needs to be said because everyone knows what they are there for, yet someone has to say and do something, and Roger managed this situation in a completely natural but meaningful way. He spoke so constructively about the game that it never seemed as though he was merely passing the time. All those three had to lead England at a difficult time, when Wales, with whom invidious comparisons would always be drawn, had a great team.

Then Billy had the captaincy thrust upon him after the return of the 1977 Lions. You could see when he started that it was far from easy for him but he again was very natural, very popular, an outstanding player. He and Roger alternated as captain, depending on the state of Roger's health, for a season or so before Billy settled into it. He learned quickly, got better and better and was outstanding in South Africa in 1980 with the Lions. In the end he led England on twenty-one occasions, a record, and was as good an international captain as you could get.

Then, of course, there was Steve Smith, who was in and out of England sides during the mid-1970s like a yo-yo yet became a very good captain. Steve's image has always been that of a joker, which he is, and I am sure that it has told against him in official circles. It was too easy to ignore the fact that he was also a very clever reader of the game and by the time he became captain, after Billy in 1982, he had the experience of twenty-two internationals behind him. England's record under his leadership reads won two, lost two, drawn one and includes a highly successful tour to North America and the massacre of Fiji. When hard words were needed he said them. I doubt if even Billy could have improved on that record and I was delighted to see Steve get the chance to captain the Lions when he was called out to New Zealand in 1983 as a replacement.

Another outstanding player was Phil Bennett, captain of Wales and of the 1977 Lions in New Zealand. He was one of three or four players during my career who were a class above their rivals, yet he remained an exceptionally nice man, a genuine family man. He would probably agree that he was not the natural choice to captain the Lions in New Zealand and his selection in that capacity probably worked against him in that it affected his own game. New Zealand never saw the best of him because when things began to go wrong he took the whole responsibility upon himself to try to get us out of trouble. In retrospect, Terry Cobner, another homely Welshman and a very good flanker, and Phil might have made a fine team as captain and vice-captain but I find it hard to criticize Phil for what happened on that tour – he did all that I could have asked of a captain.

It is more difficult passing judgement on players under whom you have not played. You can observe how teams play and, more often than not, when a team is successful an unequal share of the credit goes to the captain. Likewise, when a team fails, the captain has to be prepared to receive more than his fair share of blame. The best overseas captain during my career was Graham Mourie of New Zealand who was lucky to have an outstanding team behind him, not only of players but in management terms. He himself was a clever captain and a great player with certain physical attributes that set him apart from others: tremendous stamina and speed of reaction. In 1978 he led the All Blacks to their first grand slam in Britain and Ireland with a side managed by Russ Thomas. Russ had been one of the Lions' liaison officers in New Zealand in 1977 and I am sure he learned from the mistakes we made, particularly in public relations. He, Jack Gleeson, the 1978 coach, and Mourie appreciated that if they ignored the public face it could affect the playing performance and that the job of any tour management is to create the best atmosphere they can for players to perform in.

It could be said that those New Zealanders were conmen. Looking at their tour through a player's eyes, some of the things they said turned out not to be entirely sincere, but their public image was so good that the public believed them. They probably did no more visiting of hospitals and schools than the Lions did the year before but they got their message across and they were most helpful to the press. It was, if you like, a professional attitude to tour management and I am convinced it contributed significantly to their playing success.

7

Roses and Thorns

Some players are born to be internationals, others – of no less intrinsic worth – find themselves cast more frequently in the role of trial horse, of whom only the luckier ones break the mould and receive the reward of an international cap. Leicester, like other clubs, have had many of those reliable players whose greatest attainment may be an England trial but who rise no further. Two of them were in the side in 1975 when I began the pursuit of a third cap and a regular place in England's side – Brian Hall in the centre and Robin Cowling at loose-head prop. If anyone got the better of Brian in club matches you could start looking at him for the sort of qualities which might shine in an international context. I was very lucky to have Robin in the club front row – there was no doubt that he was one of the best props in the country, who should have been capped at a time when lesser players appeared for England. Eventually, of course, he was capped and I like to think that we helped each other in that respect, though when you consider that he was the wrong side of thirty when he finally played for England – how much the wrong side he was at pains to conceal – you could only regret the wasted seasons when he might have held down a place in the international side.

He came to us in 1974 from Gloucester and it was immediately apparent that he was a craftsman at his trade. He taught me to scrummage lower and he made my job that much easier because he was the first genuinely aggressive loose-head I had come across. The generally accepted theory was that the tight-head tried to disrupt the opposition front row while the loose-head was there to protect his own scrum ball. That was not enough for Robin. He attacked his opposing prop all the time, kept him thinking all the time and kept his mind off me. Robin's was an honest aggression – you knew exactly where you were with him and very few people tried to put one across him. He was extremely strong for a man of his size and, if the situation demanded it, he could be absolutely ruthless. He was one of those players automatically labelled 'hard', but he was not a dirty player; he was used to sorting out difficulties which referees either could not or would not notice.

It was not, however, to be his season, because he broke a leg during a squad training session. I was luckier. The visit of the touring Australians to Leicester, and subsequently of an England XV in an area trial, gave me the right exposure to reassert my claims. Free of the club captaincy I was able to concentrate on my own game but I was asked to captain the Midland Counties East in the third match of the Australian tour, under lights at Welford Road. Like so many sides which have been written off beforehand we came good and won 11–8, with a seventeen-year-old centre called Dodge playing his first big game. A month later England, attempting to build on the players who had been to Australia earlier in the year, played a Midlands and North XV which I captained, a side full of experienced club players just itching to knock over potential England players. Aided by the curious decision to leave Mike Burton on the bench, we did just that, winning 18–10.

By this time the unfortunate Burgess had gone as England coach. He needed at least a three-year term to develop the ideas with which he was brimming over and he was not given it. 'Oh ye of little faith,' he is reported to have said as he departed. It is difficult not to have sympathy with him but he needed a winning side to implement his ideas. Perhaps if he had gone more slowly, worked through the senior clubs, discussed his approach

with club coaches who had more chance of introducing it
to the players, he might have stayed. He was succeeded
by Peter Colston of Bristol, who may have seen the glow
of a false dawn when England beat Australia 23–6 (my
second match against the tourists – I was able to enjoy a
third when the Barbarians asked me to play in the final
match of the tour and I scored a try in the 19–7 win). It
was too good to be true and it may not be entirely
coincidental that I can hardly remember anything about
that international season, in which England failed to win
a championship match.

1976 was the year, too, of the incident which seems to
have exercised the minds of so many journalists since,
the game against France in Paris when I had to drop out
with a foot injury and it was afterwards hinted that I
only went along for the ride. I had received the injury
playing against the Leicestershire junior club, Westleigh,
in a qualifying game for the John Player Cup the
following season (Leicester, you will gather, had not
quite reached their cup apogee at that time). I caught a
high ball, a tackle came in and someone trod on my foot,
damaging the metatarsal. I received treatment locally
and was assured that I could play in the international if I
had a pain-killing injection, without adding further
damage. I went ahead with my plans, and on the
Thursday that we were due to travel to London to join
the England squad Garry Adey came round to my house
so that we could make the journey together. It was
Garry's second cap and he was hopping up and down
waiting to be off – but I could not find my passport. I
could not contact Margaret at school to see if she knew
where it was and eventually Garry drove off, leaving me
still searching. By the time I had found it, and driven
down to London, the scheduled training session was half
completed and Martin Cooper, the Moseley fly half, had
already failed a fitness test. The replacement was Alan
Old but the selectors overlooked him and sent for Chris
Williams of Gloucester to win his one and only cap. With
all the excitement that generated, a fitness test on my

foot was forgotten and I got through what remained of the session, though I was aware that while I could run I could not push too hard on the foot while scrummaging.

The injection will take care of that, I felt, as we left for Paris, and the next day when we trained I had the foot heavily padded and then asked Leo Walkden for an injection to make sure everything would be well the following day. That was when I discovered that RU policy was not to give injections; even if it was, Leo said, the limited area where he could inject would leave the whole foot feeling numb and me uncertain whether I had one or two feet on the ground. I went out to training with a forlorn hope but I could not possibly scrummage so it was my unpleasant task to report to the duty selector, Ron Jacobs, and tell him I would have to cry off. There was some talk of merely swapping Pullin and me round but if John had been injured and I had to come off the replacements' bench, the problem remained, so in the end my old club colleague, John Elliott, came out as the replacement and I was the sparest of spare parts. The furthest thing from my mind was the thought of conning a weekend in Paris out of the Rugby Union. It may be that if I had not been delayed reaching the Thursday training session, the whole issue would have been decided before we left England. As it turned out, I went with the squad genuinely believing I would be able to play, given an injection. It was made doubly annoying for the selectors in that the very situation they had avoided with Cooper had cropped up with me and it may be that some of them thought I had invented a cock-and-bull story about my passport in order to avoid having a fitness test.

Even so, nothing much was made of it at the time and it was only a year later, when the captaincy of England became an issue, that the theory was propounded in some newspapers that I was overlooked as a candidate because of what had happened in Paris. The journalists concerned had, presumably, heard something which hinted that, in official circles, I was regarded as unreliable. Then, every time the job of captaincy recurred, the story was trotted out, even as late as 1982 when Billy Beaumont retired. I suppose, human nature being what it is, an incident such as that might have had some effect when the captaincy was being discussed in 1977 but surely it had no bearing five or six years later. If the Rugby Union felt I would have gone to such lengths just to get a weekend in Paris they can have had little regard for me as a person, but I would have hoped that, during the next six years, I had shown other qualities which might have eradicated any such impression.

The season, however, was not a total disaster because I did feel, at the end of it, that I was recognized as England's regular hooker. I had come of age as an international. I found in club games that while some players treated me with a certain respect, others would deliberately have a go at me just because I was an England player. Privilege of rank perhaps, though it was quite amusing to find that referees sometimes tended to give you the benefit of the doubt: where before they might have given a penalty for foot up, now just once or twice I think I might have got away with a quick strike because, as an international, I was supposed to be good.

The Barbarians too were there with a pick-me-up during the summer of 1976, when they chose Garry and me for their tour to North America and Canada. I am permanently grateful to the Baa-baas for their considerate treatment of me throughout my career. We have an excellent relationship with them, in any case, because of Leicester's annual fixture, and I had got to know their officers well when I was club captain and involved in the speech-making. They helped me back into the limelight in 1974, they chose me as the only Englishman in the side against Australia in 1976 and they were a tonic that summer after a succession of losing England games. Perhaps significantly, too, there were a number of our players hoping for places in the 1977 Lions tour to New Zealand and I was one of them. It was great to play for England yet the ultimate honour for any player is to represent the Lions. Seven of those Barbarians were to tour in New Zealand, an eighth was selected but could not go and three more became Lions in 1980. The Barbarians captain, Phil Bennett, also led the 1977 Lions though on tour in Canada I was given the privilege of leading the Baa-baas against Alberta – a match distinguished by my request to the referee to blow for time early, not because we were exhausted but because we had scored over fifty points and it was no part of our intentions on tour to rub people's noses in the mud.

It would be fair to say that we were probably not as fit as we might have been for that tour. We had a strong party, it was partly a flag-waving mission and we were not stretched to win all our games. North America is a superb place to tour too – there is always something to do and many of those who were in New Zealand the following year must have watched the rain sluicing down out of a grey New Zealand sky and thought back to those days with the Barbarians. Geoff Wheel, the Swansea lock, proved the star turn of the Barbarians tour, accompanied by his little banjo. He would get everyone singing then hurl the instrument away into a corner when the atmosphere became a little hectic – but the banjo would always turn up safe and sound because someone could always be relied upon to pick it up and restore it to the team baggage. Just to show what an enthusiast he was for training too, Geoff heaved the exercise cycle from the sports hall to the hotel sauna one afternoon, determined to lose some weight – as he pedalled away the steam was practically coming out of his ears.

If I have enjoyed some very good times with the Barbarians, the same may be said of the Irish Wolfhounds, roughly speaking Ireland's equivalent guest team. I have played for the Wolf hounds several times as they go about their self-appointed task of taking first-class players away from the cities to the smaller clubs whose view of international players is usually confined to the television or a spectator's ticket at Lansdowne Road.

Their habit is to invite young and promising Irishmen to play alongside leading players from the other international championship countries against junior clubs who are permitted their own guest players for the day. They do a splendid job for Irish rugby and the welcome they extend to 'foreigners' is exceptionally warm, and never better than the time Paul Dodge, Les Cusworth and I were invited to play for the Wolf hounds near Sligo, shortly after Lord Mountbatten had been killed when a terrorist bomb blew up his motorboat. It was little short of a standing ovation.

It was back to the real world in September 1976, and the new challenge presented by Argentina. It was a challenge limited to only one game in England – the rest were in Wales – and a North and Midlands XV met the Argentinians in Leicester. It was an exceptionally strong combined side, captained by Cotton, yet we were not rated too highly because the Argentinians had come through their three games in Wales without losing. Eleven of the North and Midlands players were involved in England's grand slam season of 1980, which does serve to show what might have been if they had been brought together on England's behalf earlier on. Chalkie White prepared the side at two sessions, one in the north and one at Leicester on the day before the game. We set out to play a limited game with the following side: Dusty Hare, John Carleton, Paul Dodge, Tony Bond, Mike Slemen, John Horton, Steve Smith, Fran Cotton, Peter Wheeler, Colin White, Dick Trickey, Bill Beaumont, David Forfar, Garry Adey, Tony Neary. We were strong up front, we had two big centres to knock down the speedy Argentinian runners and we had Dusty to kick the goals. He did, five penalties and a conversion, and we won 24–9, only to be heavily criticized that same evening by Dick Jeeps, then president of the Rugby Union, for our negative play.

I found it astonishing that we should have to face such criticism. In a dream world we would all happily play to the wings but in the real world, with limited time in which to prepare, you play to your own strength, not the opposition strength. It is not even true to say that any team playing the way we did could have won and if you start running the ball all over the place against a national side which has had a little time to get together, and you come unstuck, it is extremely difficult to dig your way out. If Chalkie had had our side together over a number of games – and I am sure he would have loved to – then we could have developed a style, the style that eventually brought England the grand slam. As it was the Argentinians returned to Wales and lost to a Welsh XV the next week – by one point.

Argentina have proved, since then, that they are a force to be reckoned with, though they are not yet quite consistent enough. At the same time it may not be fully appreciated that it is a considerable achievement to go into a game with a specific plan and come off the field having played to that plan. Fifteen other blokes and an odd-shaped ball keep doing their best to get in the way of your plan. I would agree that it is more difficult to go out to play free-flowing rugby because the risk element is considerable, but we were proud that we had achieved what we set out to do. I am sorry the feelings of the players and their coach on that occasion were not shared by the alickadoos.

I was delighted that, when the England team to meet Scotland was announced, Robin Cowling was in it. It was a just reward and it coincided with an emphatic win in the Calcutta Cup match. We were all conscious of the need to do well and earn selection for the Lions and, though you cannot play an international championship season as though it were a build-up for a long tour, a good start certainly helps. Scotland were at a low ebb; some of their forwards were coming to the end of a long road and their most influential player, Gordon Brown, the lock, had been suspended. Scotland needed someone of his stature to build on but they had no one. England, after the 1976 season in which we lost all four games, were cautious and playing to a limited plan, much of which operated round the big Rosslyn Park centre, Charles Kent, who would plough back into the forwards to set up secondary ball. We concentrated on eliminating mistakes, Roger Uttley did a fine job as captain and we were lucky in that our first two games were 'second-division matches', at a time when critics tended to divide the championship into first division (France and Wales) and second division (the other three countries). We went to Ireland for the next game and came away with another win, which induced the kind of confidence so lacking in the previous two years.

In we went against France, whose grand slam year this was. They had a tremendous pack, big, intimidating, aggressive. They had specialists for every position who knew exactly what they had to do. Imbernon and Palmié were not there to catch line-out ball, that was the job of the giant Bastiat. The two locks were there as donkeys in the scrum, to hit the rucks and mauls and to disrupt our line-out as much as possible. Cholley and Paparemborde were two good props and, like their hooker, Paco, good in the loose too. There were two world-class flankers, Rives and Skrela, backed up by little Fouroux at scrum half and Romeu to kick goals. We lost (4–3) and were unlucky to do so. We had our chances to win the game, particularly in the matter of goal-kicking, but Alastair Hignell, for all his defensive virtues, did not have the consistency of a Hare when it came to kicking.

But the result did mean we had come a long way forward in a year and we went down to Wales for the triple crown game. Before the game in Cardiff John Dawes, the Welsh coach, made all the right noises to the press: England, he said, must be favourites after their strong performance against France, Wales were worried. It was a load of rubbish – very, very few sides go to Cardiff as favourites. Unfortunately some people believed him and there were even some quotes from our camp which suggested we fancied our chances. We lost. It may have been only 14–9 but it was decisive enough. England may have frozen slightly and we were well

96

beaten among the forwards, Gareth Edwards and J. P. R. Williams scored the only tries of the game, and a lot of arguments regarding selection for the Lions were resolved. It may, for instance, have been that match which took Clive Williams into the Lions party at loose-head prop and caused Cowling's omission.

When the party to tour New Zealand was named it included sixteen Welshmen. Two more subsequently joined the tour as replacements. At that stage I was naive enough to believe still that selectors always know what they are doing. I have no doubt that Dawes, as coach to the side and with a tremendous reputation as captain of the only Lions party to win a series in New Zealand, exerted a lot of pressure on behalf of the Welsh players, even though it was known beforehand that several of the great names – Edwards, Gerald Davies, Mervyn Davies (whose career had been terminated through injury) – would not be available. As an outsider you tended to take for granted that some of the lesser Welsh lights selected would live up to their promise. Not all of them did so but I was in no mood to analyse the tour party. I was in it. It was all I had wanted from rugby and it made a marvellous end to what had been a not unsatisfactory season. The party was: Andy Irvine, Bruce Hay, Peter Squires, Elgan Rees, John J. Williams, Gareth Evans, Mike Gibson, Steve Fenwick, David Burcher, Ian McGeechan, Phil Bennett, John Bevan, Brynmor Williams, Douglas Morgan, Fran Cotton, Phil Orr, Bobby Windsor, Peter Wheeler, Graham Price, Clive Williams, Nigel Horton, Moss Keane, Allan Martin, Gordon Brown, Jeff Squire, Tony Neary, Trevor Evans, Terry Cobner, Willie Duggan, Derek Quinnell. Later additions to the party were Billy Beaumont, Charlie Faulkner and Alun Lewis.

It was the final step on the ladder to acceptance as a player of international stature, an acceptance which has sometimes meant that others may regard you as the fount of all knowledge. So many people have asked me for tips about hooking and I find it difficult to oblige. Not because I do not want to pass on my experience but because it is one of those positions where you really have to learn for yourself, to work out your own answers to the problems that confront you. There are so many variables: different physical shapes, different strengths, different leverages, and what may suit one player, because of the front row in which he finds himself, may not suit another. The one imperative for any aspiring hooker is simple: he must win his own ball.

Nowadays it is customary for the hooker to signal to his scrum half when he is ready for the ball to be put in, by lifting his hand. This is known as 'flapping'. When I began there was no such system. It was introduced, I believe, by one of the university sides who were finding it difficult to cope with heavier, more experienced club packs and therefore adopted this system in the hope of gaining a split-second advantage. Those university grants aren't wasted after all! It was taken up by most other sides though I did not begin flapping until 1980 when I was playing with Terry Holmes for the Lions. He was used to watching his hooker's hand rather than the tunnel of the scrum so I conformed to his system – then he was injured and had to be replaced. Poor Terry. In the first test against New Zealand in 1983 he was penalized for interfering with a prop who seemed to be preventing Cieran Fitzgerald from flapping and later, in the same match, received an injury which again sent him home from a Lions tour early.

In the beginning, playing for the old boys, we had a reasonable front row and sometimes managed an astronomical number of strikes against the head, because it was a matter of whose reaction was quickest. The hooker reacted to the scrum half's hands moving and, of course, since we had no coaching system and seemed to be getting on well enough by ourselves, nobody attempted to teach me to hook or told me how I might improve.

When I moved to Leicester I discovered that a major difference between the junior game and the first-class is that the higher your playing level, the lower the scrum tends to be, until it gets to the point where you can hardly bring your foot across to strike for the ball and end up kicking it away in the wrong direction. You have to learn to cope with that. In fact, all front-row play is a question of coping with whatever the opposition has in store for you. I had to learn in the hard school, against hookers who, whatever their ability about the field, were very quick strikers for the ball, as most hookers who played during the fifties and sixties were. I learned against characters like John Pullin and Andy Johnson (who sometimes got the better of me), against the Welsh, against the Gloucester front row at Kingsholm, and against props who were very quick with their feet, like Mike Burton and Keith Fairbrother. I had everything thrown against me in the front row and you learn very quickly or it is difficult to survive. Among the first things you learn is that the front rows establish their own ground rules because parts of play are not covered by the laws of the game and if the referee is not going to supply the answer to your particular problem – and very often he can't, poor man, because he does not know what's going on either – you have to work out your own answers.

As a young hooker, you talk as much as you can to the opposition in the natural course of the post-match badinage, or when buying your opposite number a drink. You are unlikely to discuss the game just played; more likely you will discuss other front rows and how you have both coped with them. You never concede that anything that day's opponent might have done inconvenienced you at all. The first time I played against Mike Burton we were both in our respective clubs' second teams; the second time was in the senior side, when Gloucester were fielding an exeptionally good front row of Burton, Mike Nicholls and Cowling. In those days I was young and innocent and prepared to have a go for balls against the head. I did so once and the next time I tried it, the scrum broke up and I took a terrific crack on the jaw. Burton had hit me and it took me some moments to realize it was because I had had the cheek to try to steal their scrum ball. On another occasion I turned my head to look down the tunnel for the ball when Burton turned his head and opened his mouth, as if to bite me. He did not sink his fangs in like some latter-day Dracula, but the trick fooled me and I looked away just as the ball came in. I had naturally lost a vital moment's concentration and I have to admit that he tried the same ruse successfully several other times. Like all front rows, he remembered the tricks that work and when we next played against each other he knew it was worth trying again. This time I had an answer worked out: as he turned his head, I turned mine as if to bite him back. Not a pretty thought and, since I was not wearing a gum shield, he got a mouthful of toothless gum in his face and he never tried it on again. That, though it does not sound entirely pleasant, is the essence of front-row play, and after a while, when you have been on the first-class circuit long enough, there is no need to go through the repertoire of tricks; you can both get on and play the game. It is only when there is an unknown factor, some new player whom you have not previously encountered, that the jousting goes on and then you may find some kind of flare-up in the front row. No front-row forward can afford to allow the opposition to intimidate him in any way, physically or verbally, and a quick eruption may be the only way to sort it out. Then the wise referee does not make a song-and-dance about it, because the players have done the job for him. Only when the referee is sure of his ground should he take decisive action.

When your experience is still limited you may go into games with a certain amount of apprehension, particularly against Welsh or West Country opponents. Stories abound about the tricks of hardened Welsh props and if you have never taken a right hook to the jaw, or suffered some kind of cut requiring stitches, a certain fear of the unknown must remain. I have no wish to frighten people away from the game or stop parents from encouraging their children to play, but it would be idle to pretend that this kind of confrontation does not go on. Much of it looks worse than it is; you learn that, when the fists are flying, 95 per cent of the blows aimed never connect. You may have, as I did, a cut which needs seventeen stitches on the side of the head and you discover that though there is a lot of blood, it does not hurt that much, you get a lot of sympathy and your head is still firmly attached to your shoulders.

In that situation you may well find, too, that your captain is playing a psychological game just as much as the front rows. 'Don't worry,' he'll say as you crawl out from beneath a maul, blood in your eyes and not sure whether it is day or night, 'it's only a scratch, the sponge man will sort it out.' He knows, as well as anyone, that in a tight game few surface injuries are so serious that they cannot wait for another twenty minutes. The 'kidology' will recur perhaps if you have a new forward. We took a young lock down to Gloucester and, during the game, won a scrum near their posts. 'Don't hit him here, it'll cost us three points,' grunted a West Country voice – Burton once again. Our lad was off and away as soon as the scrum broke up and that was what Burton wanted to know. He could judge from that reaction that at least one Leicester player would be worrying all the time about whether a punch was coming through and that, there-fore, he could not be concentrating on the game as much as he should.

It was all part of growing up, in rugby terms. It sounds rough, sometimes it is, but if it was all as bad as it is sometimes made out to be very few of us would stay playing five, ten, fifteen years in the game. An initial difficulty for youngsters just beginning their careers is the fact that you cannot train, as a hooker, by yourself, so the more team training and match practice you get, the better. What you can do is develop your upper body strength through weight training, though in fact I found that this happened naturally the more I continued scrummaging. The hooker has to have strength across the shoulders, in the neck and also in the arms, for binding. He has to be prepared to do a lot of running and he can practise throwing in at a line-out. It is likely that if you have two hookers of similar ability, and one is a more accurate thrower than the other, he is the one who will win the senior place. Again, throwing at a post or a mark on a wall is not the same as throwing to a jumper, where speed, timing and style of throw – lobbed, flat or whatever – can be developed. Nothing beats experience.

As far as defending your own ball is concerned, you have to get your left foot as far across to the edge of the tunnel as you can and bind as well as you can. That having been said, you must always remember your basic objective, that of winning your own ball, and if that means having to loosen the bind on the right hand it may be necessary to do so. I always found it better to be tightly bound because you are in a better position to defend against an eight-man shove. On the opposition ball you must put them under pressure as much as possible. You may attempt to strike against the head, which these days is rare; you may be pushing, be attempting to wheel, you may dummy an attempt to strike and try for a foot-up verdict against them, you may keep your own feet right back and try to squeeze a not-straight decision from the referee. The one thing you must never do is allow them a free shot at the ball because the ideal situation for any hooker is to be under no pressure and free to choose how he channels the ball to the best advantage for his scrum half. You must concentrate, you must organize the people around you so that they do everything in their power to make your job as comfortable as possible, because yours is the ultimate responsibility for winning the ball. You can never reach a scrummage looking for a rest; if two or three forwards are taking a breather and the opposition produce an eight-man shove, you will find yourself going backwards very rapidly.

Watch your opponents all the time; you may get a clue about their intentions from the position of their hooker's feet and be better prepared to resist when the time comes. How the ball is channelled depends on the move being planned by the halfbacks or back row; the only really quick ball is that which emerges between second row and flanker and even then you must be careful that the opposing scrum half does not come through on an unprotected ball. People talk, sometimes a bit glibly, of channel one, two or three but when you are in an international the last thing you think about is hitting the ball five degrees one way or another, at this or that speed. It is unrealistic, particularly when you consider the immense pressure exerted by an international pack of forwards. You find yourself back once more at home base: win your own ball.

I have been very lucky in my international career to have played in some of the great forward packs, two of which had the benefit of coming together on a tour, when every aspect of play is honed to the finest edge. There was the 1977 Lions pack in New Zealand, England's grand slam pack in 1980 and the Lions pack in South Africa the same year. If I had to pick one of those three I would say that England's pack in 1980 just shaded the 1977 Test pack, possibly because – strange though it may seem to talk about New Zealanders in such terms – in 1977 they seemed short of quality props. Referees in New Zealand seldom let the scrums go down until the ball was ready to be put in and they were very lenient about scrum halves feeding the ball crooked. There was no competition; you must remember that Cotton and Graham Price were at their peak in 1977 and that we had two grafting locks, Billy Beaumont and Gordon Brown, and two very competitive flankers, Terry Cobner and Derek Quinnell, all pushing their weight. In 1980 England had Cotton and another immensely strong man, Phil Blakeway, as loose-head and tight-head, Beaumont and Maurice Colclough at lock, Neary and Uttley on the flanks with John Scott at number eight. It was a tremendous pack and, interestingly enough, one which was rated very highly by another outstanding prop, Robert Paperemborde of France.

103

The French were another side who would always put you on your mettle, assuming that is that their selectors had not suffered one of their periodic aberrations. The French pack from the team which won the grand slam in 1977 was immensely strong, the best I ever played against, and all of them specialists in their positions. The French in 1983 were good too, and they included Philippe Dintrans whom I rate as the best hooker I ever played against. I am prepared to forgive him the occasional lapse as a thrower at the line-out; there were times when he really did not have much to throw to in the way of jumpers.

Generally speaking it is hookers I have encountered at home who provided the best opposition. Andy Dalton of New Zealand, particularly on tour in 1978, was a good player, but New Zealand have not produced so many good technicians and the South Africans tend to rely on very big men who push their weight but are not quick strikers. I always had a lot of time for Bobby Windsor of Wales. He was consistently difficult to play against, he was quick around the field and so many Welsh moves started with him at ruck or maul.

But even allowing for the international sides which have provided so much satisfaction, memories of the 1981 John Player Cup final will always bring a smile. It was Leicester's third successive cup win and came against a Gosforth side which, if you believed all you read in the papers, was going to scrummage us off Twickenham. It has been a favourite pastime to discount Leicester packs but we have always been capable of a special effort when we knew it was required. We knew we needed one that day and then we discovered that the Gosforth pack was not operating at 100 per cent. Suddenly we found ourselves not just holding them but dominating them and we were able to produce our best cup-final win.

Everyone enjoys picking their favourite team. I shall content myself with naming the props I should like to have at my side if ever I find myself scrummaging for my life – only I shall cheat and pick a reserve front row too! This is an exercise like *Desert Island Discs*. I have no doubt that once the castaway on the desert island has sweated his way to his eight favourite records, all the other haunting tunes he has ever known come home to plague him. In an ideal world I would have at my side Fran Cotton, Graham Price, Phil Blakeway and Robin Cowling and if, for some reason, I could not play or needed a spot of scrummaging practice, I would have Philippe Dintrans available to hook against. Robin may have lacked the stature of the other three props but he would die before conceding ground. Come to think of it, he must have felt he was dying when he propped against France in 1978 with a dislocated shoulder because both our replacements had been used. He was that kind of man.

8

From Tigers to Lions

The tour of the Lions through New Zealand in 1977, with its trials, tribulations and bitter disappointments, has been well documented, so I will content myself with a strictly personal impression. It was the tour on which I reached my highest peak as a player yet, paradoxically, suffered my lowest ebb during a first-class career covering fourteen years. My knowledge of New Zealand rugby was limited to what I had read of the 1971 tour and two brief encounters with Ian Kirkpatrick's New Zealanders of 1972–73 and Andy Leslie's tourists of 1974 but nothing can prepare you properly save a visit to the country itself. Even when you reach New Zealand you can go up and down the country and discover how different areas emphasize different aspects of the game. In Otago, for instance, they play rugby like nowhere else on earth. The ruck is all in their game and they perform it in a way I never met elsewhere in New Zealand. Nothing seems to make them happier than to set up ruck after ruck, and if the eventual consequence is a score it almost appears incidental.

I was luckier in accepting the invitation to tour than some other members of the party. My firm appreciated my long-term commitment to rugby and gave me paid leave of absence; like so many other employers they hope to get their pound of flesh when my playing days are over. Someone like Clive Williams, the Welsh prop, was not so lucky; his employers were prepared to keep his job open for him but not to pay him while he was in New Zealand. His club and his friends rallied round to make sure that his wife could pay the mortgage while he was away but Clive could hardly have been anything but uncomfortable at accepting what was, in effect, charity. Dougie Morgan, Scotland's scrum half, was a self-employed chiropodist; he had either to close his business while he was in New Zealand and possibly lose a good many of his clients or pay for a locum. Meanwhile the tour itself made a profit of £1 million. The profit-sacrifice equation does not make sense to me and I shall return to it.

You develop tremendous relationships with other players on long tours. National identities quickly become submerged beneath the need to do well for the Lions and, in the sense that you are a party of thirty-two in what may be termed hostile territory – and at times it is literally that – thousands of miles from home, you learn much more about your colleagues under stress. You play with them, you live with them day in and day out. You room with nearly everyone, you see players demonstrating raw courage in head-on tackles or diving for the ball at the feet of an All Black pack. It seems grotesque to compare it with warfare but I have no doubt that the atmosphere before the second Test against New Zealand was very much like that in the trenches of the First World War, before the soldiers went over the top to face the German barrage. It must be wrong to equate men risking their lives with thirty people playing a game, but it was that kind of intense feeling. And, in those circumstances, a certain camaraderie grows up. You are all faced with the same criticisms, the same living problems, and it is impossible to hide or to pretend. Basically shy people begin to blossom when some incident brings out the hidden depths in their characters. In the low moments you find yourself discussing things with relative strangers which normally you would only disclose to your wife or close family.

In that respect, I suppose, your party becomes something like a large, overgrown family. Inevitably, as in any family, there are quarrels but at bottom we nearly all got along well and respected each other. The tour cemented relationships for me with other England players – with Cotton, with Beaumont who joined the tour very much as junior lock forward just as I was second-choice hooker at the start, with Neary and with the Harrogate wing, Peter Squires. It also established new relationships with players who, previously, had been opponents. I enjoyed the company of the uncapped Cardiff scrum half, Brynmor Williams, and Derek Quinnell of Llanelli, with whom I organized match tickets for the players. Though much of the criticism which followed the tour was directed at the management, I enjoyed touring with George Burrell and John Dawes too. Burrell, a former Scottish fullback, I found a very likeable man though, as manager, he may have allowed Dawes too much freedom in his coaching role. Some of the senior players did not get on with them quite so readily but my own feeling for Dawes was one of respect for what he had achieved as a player, captain and coach. Perhaps what it all boiled down to was that they were as much members of the party as the players; they were at the sharp end fielding all the problems as they grew around us. All the flak that came their way was from 'outsiders'.

New Zealand I soon discovered to be a land of contrasts. From the first match onwards there was a sense of hostility emanating from New Zealanders in the mass. It even came over again, six years later, watching recorded highlights of the 1983 tour on television, the almost tangible fervour of a New Zealand crowd hoping to see the Lions thrashed. They feel more for their sport there than anywhere else in the world, possibly because it is the one sport where they are world leaders and because it is the sport which for so long typified the rugged masculinity with which so many New Zealanders identified. And, most importantly, when we arrived they were hungry for success. We flew out with a considerable weight of expectation on our shoulders, the first Lions party in history to travel as favourites after the successes of 1971 and 1974. New Zealand, by contrast, had lost in

South Africa in 1970 and 1976; they had lost at home in 1971 and endured a poor tour of Britain in 1972–73. Whatever they may have achieved against other countries, the highlight for New Zealanders is a game between All Blacks and Lions, or All Blacks and Springboks. Those only occur once every five or six years in New Zealand while we in Britain are accustomed to our regular four home championship matches.

So while individual New Zealanders could hardly do enough for us – and I made some good friends on that tour – hostility welled out of the impersonal crowds and through the popular press (not that certain journals were very popular with us). Every weekend we found the New Zealand press hanging some albatross round our necks and not only on the sports pages. In Britain we seldom look for sport on the front page but there they were, the screaming page-one headlines, the lurid stories. 'Lions are animals', an everyday story of provincial players whose careers had come to an abrupt end because of acts of unmitigated violence from the Lions. It was complete fabrication but the mud sticks. 'Lions are louts' told of the Lions smashing up a hotel and throwing other guests into the swimming pool. 'Lions are lousy lovers' was the confession of the local Juliet who, claiming intimate knowledge of several Lions players, was well-placed to proclaim that she preferred New Zealanders in her bed. One journal – I hesitate to call it a newspaper – ran a series entitled 'Animal of the Week', which award went one week to Cotton after an alleged short-arm tackle.

It was not only the papers. The incidents happened in games too. There was the occasion when the front rows were about to go down and a full can of beer came hurtling from the crowd, just missing us. In another match J.J. Williams, the Welsh wing, was forced into touch and promptly had beer thrown into his face before he could get back onto the field. At the end of the second test, which we won, I was about to leave the field when I heard a voice calling me for help. It was Brynmor Williams who was being set upon by one of the crowd who had come streaming onto the pitch after the final whistle.

In the face of the accumulating hostility, the automatic reaction is to close ranks. From beginning with an open-minded attitude to the bevy of journalists who always accompany a major tour, you find yourself catching your tongue when off-the-cuff remarks find their way into the papers and are quoted completely out of context. You find information appearing in the papers that could only have been acquired from some official in close contact with the tour party. And when some of the less sensational stories begin to appear in British papers, queries arise in letters from home or in telephone calls which only add to the concern. I appreciate that journalists have stories to file and deadlines to meet and that a certain amount of the animosity which arose between press and party on that tour was due to poor public relations by the management. If the Lions themselves did not provide what might be called the 'party line', the media must go digging for it themselves. I was interested to see on the current tour that two of the Lions had been permitted to help with a guest column for one of the New Zealand weeklies, which shows that some lessons have been learned since 1977. Our management felt that they did not get the support from the British press that they deserved but they may not have worked hard enough to earn that support. The press, and this is intended as no discredit to them, can be manipulated reasonably easily, as the All Blacks showed all too clearly when they toured in Britain in 1978. Perhaps Burrell and Dawes expected it as a right.

No natural division into Saturday and Wednesday sides had appeared in the party before the first Test at Wellington so the competition for places in the international was fierce, with no clues available about who would be successful. I began the tour as number two to Bobby Windsor, who had played in all four Tests in South Africa for the Lions in 1974. He had much more experience than I at that stage so I dare say it was reasonable to assume he was the likely hooker at Wellington, though I would never have made that assumption. I was picked to play in the side against New Zealand Universities on the Tuesday before the Test, which suggested that Bobby would play on the Saturday – and when we lost to the students, possibility became probability. We did not play well, we deserved to lose, and it did not help to raise my spirits when the side to play New Zealand was announced the following day and I was not in it. That same day we underwent the savage training session which has passed into rugby legend. It went on and on until all you wanted to do was lie down and never get up again. At the time it seemed to be Dawes's way of punishing us for losing to the universities, though defeat had nothing to do with lack of fitness. It was the hardest session I have ever undertaken, though we had something approaching it in South Africa in 1980.

The next stage of what was rapidly turning out to be not my day was the flight to Wellington, and when we arrived all any of us wanted to do was sleep. But I had been asked to be guest speaker at the Cartertown Rugby Club that evening, which was a car drive of some one and a half hours from Wellington. It is not difficult to imagine how I felt having, over the previous twenty-four hours, played in a losing side, had a few beers in the evening, suffered the mental let-down of missing the first international, suffered at training and travelled to Wellington. Now I piled into a car, was driven to a small village hall where I knew no one, performed the social niceties and was then driven back to the hotel bedroom which was all I had wanted. Apologies, Cartertown Rugby Club, if I did not come up to scratch.

It was an unhappy day, yet it was during that week that an outstanding victory in the second Test was born. Several of the forwards got together in the bar one evening to discuss what was going wrong with the tour. Cobner was there, so was I and half a dozen others and it was after that episode that 'Cobs' began to take responsibility for the forwards. Defeat in the first Test added point to our talk-in. It has been said, with hindsight, that we left our form in that Wellington test behind us on the training field. I do not go along with that entirely because the first Test turned on an interception made by Grant Batty when the Lions looked likely to score and establish a respectable lead. But defeat meant that we all knew we could not afford to lose the next game in the series or the tour would be heading for the rocks. We would have been away from home for two months with nothing to show for it, and we would have to put up with another six weeks in New Zealand being told we were 'no-hopers'. More constructively, those of us who had missed the first Test knew there were places going in the second. There were five matches between the two Tests which gave us time to establish a place in the important games, against Canterbury and Wellington. You can tell how seriously we all took it when, during the week following our Test defeat, we were all in bed by ten o'clock.

I played in the midweek game at Timaru, against South/Mid Canterbury and North Otago and Bobby played against Canterbury. But my hopes rose when he was picked for the next game, against West Coast-Buller, and I found myself playing against Wellington, one of the leading provincial sides and led by the former New Zealand captain, Andy Leslie. We did well to win 13–6 and when the team for the second Test was announced after the game against Marlborough-Nelson Bays, Bobby was out and I was in. He was the first to offer congratulations. It is difficult to describe my feelings at having won the Test place. Bobby himself remarked that touring with the Lions is great if you are winning, if you steer clear of injury and if you are in the Test team. You all go through the same work, the same preparation, but only half the party gets the reward of playing in the big games. I had always got on well with Bobby, there was mutual respect between us. Like so many Welshmen he was very down-to-earth, a great family man, and enjoyed company, but while we were the best of friends, there was always an element of reserve because no matter how well you get on with someone, it is always your ambition to be in the top side instead of him. That apart, however, he helped me a lot, there was always healthy competition between us in training but neither of us felt we had anything to prove to the other which, I think, is something common to most rugby people. I knew he was better than me in some areas of play, he knew the reverse was true but we never felt the need to rub it in. The contest was keen but clean.

The dressing room before the second Test, which was played at Christchurch, was a place I can never forget. The emotion was oozing out of the walls. We were far from home, we had been castigated up and down New Zealand. Then there was Phil Bennett and 'Cobs', stripping away any remaining element of reserve, laying it all on the line: victory was not only for ourselves, it was for our friends, our supporters, our families who were getting up in the middle of the night back in Britain to follow our progress on the radio. Don't let them down, boys. We didn't. It was close, it was extremely physical, it was no advertisement for rugby and we could have lost it near the end. But we won 13–9; Phil kicked three penalties for us, Bryan Williams kicked three for them and J.J. scored the try that made the difference. The account in *Rothmans Rugby Yearbook* says: 'the cohesion and spirit displayed by the [Lions] forwards decided the issue.' It also says: 'Isolated outbreaks of violence, the worst caused by the late charge on Bennett, did nothing for rugby.' The feeling of victory was more intense than when England won the grand slam three years later. That was a progressive achievement and by the time we came to the final leg, against Scotland, we were nearly home and dry. The second Test was hard from beginning to end and victory was dredged out of defeat. The celebrations afterwards were something to remember and the next day we were summoned to the room of our faithful and friendly New Zealand baggage man, 'Doc'

Murdoch, to take our medicine. The 'medicine' turned out to be the hair of the dog and the singing and celebration began again during Sunday.

The week that followed was like nothing I had ever experienced, or ever hope to experience again. I regard myself as an even-tempered sort of person, not much given to great peaks or troughs of emotion, but during the week after the second Test I went through an appalling depression. Obviously it was a reflection of the emotional 'high' we all reached going into the game at Christchurch, and several of the players I spoke to later said they too experienced a similar depression. I found it hard to cope with and the lowest point was reached after the next game I played, against Waikato. It was a hard niggly game which we won 18–13 and as we were going down into one scrum on halfway – just in front of the television cameras – their hooker, 'Foxy' Bennett, brought his knee up into my face. I was not wearing a gum shield and it knocked a tooth out; Clive Williams was unluckier because he received an injury which finished his tour. During the post-match reception I went outside by myself and sat on a bench, and felt that I would not have cared if I never saw a rugby ball again. Why on earth was I there, thousands of miles from home, getting my teeth kicked in? Two or three days in some dentist's chair to get my mouth sorted out on top of everything else that had plagued the tour. Like the weather. It was still raining. People unconnected with rugby may ask what I had to grumble about. I was seeing another country at someone else's expense, pursuing my favourite hobby, being well looked after. But when you find yourself at yet another up-country town, so small a thing as the weather can haunt you. We would play in the rain; we would get up for training on the Monday morning, and it would rain. We would go back to the hotel for lunch and try to dry our kit. There was no chance of golf or swimming because of the rain so you drift down to the local snooker hall in the afternoon. In the evening there is nowhere to go because everywhere is closed and the only open bar in town is the one in the team hotel and you know perfectly well that if you go into the public bar there will be the fingers wagging in your face, telling you – and anyone else who cares to listen – just where the tour is going wrong and how you compare with the 'greats' of 1950, 1959 or 1971. You go to bed and get up the next day to find your kit is still damp; you struggle into it for training and still the rain pours down. You can put up with that sort of routine for two or three weeks but after two solid months of it, there develops a certain weariness with the world. That was how I felt. It may sound ungrateful, and it may be that, in other circumstances, we should have felt much more outgoing towards the local people. But you can only react to the circumstances in which you find yourself and, on that bench in Waikato, I felt the world had closed in. Margaret told me later, when I was back home, that my letters during that period made her feel New Zealand was the worst country in the world and that all we wanted to do was beat the All Blacks and get out fast. The old-timers will say how much longer they spent away from home, when tours to New Zealand took six months. But much of that time was taken up by the boat trip out and back and I doubt if they were subjected to the same pressure from the media, with every aspect of the party's doings scrutinized to the nth degree.

The second Test win did mean, statistically at any rate, that the tour was back on the rails. The forwards had improved dramatically but the backs, who had looked in good form before the first Test, were not in such good order. Perhaps, of all of us, they felt the rain and the constant criticism most. New Zealanders expect to see exciting back play from the Lions; they look back fondly to the giants of other years, to Bleddyn Williams, Lewis and Ken Jones in 1950, to Bev Risman, Ken Scotland and David Hewitt in 1959, to Edwards, John, Gibson and the rest in 1971. We had no one of that stature in 1977 or, to put it another way, no one developed that kind of stature. The Mike Gibson of 1977

115

was not the same player as the Mike Gibson of 1971; maybe he was never given the opportunity to be. But we never quite overcame the problems at half-back where Brynmor Williams, talented player though he undoubtedly was, could not overcome his own lack of confidence. He spent so many years, for Cardiff and Wales, in the shadow of Gareth Edwards that when he was given his place in the limelight he was nervous of exploiting his own ability to the full. I think he constantly compared himself with Gareth, worrying about whether he was living up to the great man, and then injury in the form of a damaged hamstring bit into his play. Even in our lighter moments we could not avoid some kind of misfortune because I have a feeling that Brynmor accentuated the strain when trying to avoid the snapping claws of a live lobster which Steve Fenwick introduced to the hotel one day.

Nor did we see the best of Phil Bennett on that tour. His brilliance emerged in flashes but it remained under a cloud during the Test matches as he became more and more depressed with his own form, as injury and the strains of captaincy took their toll. But Phil was a great man, never better than when the team got together after a match, by ourselves, for a 'nostalgia' hour. We would sing all the old songs, talk about games we had played in, Phil would sing 'Swansea Town' and any problems just drifted away. It was not always the 'bad news' tour. We had great fun at Nigel Starmer-Smith's expense one day when he was interviewing Derek Quinnell for *Rugby Special* and suddenly a gorilla's face peered out of the bushes straight into the eye of the camera. It was Allan Martin equipped with a mask; the rest of us restrained our mirth so that Derek could tell a slightly embarrassed Nigel just how we were going to beat New Zealand.

On the field, the mirthful moments were few. Phil was obviously a marked man and the subject of endless late tackles. He seldom received any protection from the referees and how he came through the tour in one piece I shall never know. His players would have done anything for him. During the second Test he kicked to clear his line and the ball was just spiralling into touch when Kevin Eveleigh, the New Zealand flanker, hit him with a late tackle. I just saw red and laid into Eveleigh in a way I have never done anywhere else. The electric atmosphere in which that game was played may have had something to do with it and the incident gave rise to a much-featured photograph in which Sid Going is holding me while Eveleigh aims a punch.

It must be said though that, however dubious their methods occasionally were, the All Blacks completely closed Phil down. I could only have immense respect for the tactical awareness of Jack Gleeson, the New Zealand coach, after that second Test. He saw the writing on the wall for New Zealand's forwards and changed his side's style of play. He dropped Going for Lyn Davis, a scrum half who would spread the ball wide. He brought in a new fullback and two new three-quarters, a new prop and a new flanker, Graham Mourie. He recognized that the Lions' strength lay in their pack but that the back row, without Neary, lacked pace about the field, so he picked backs who could use the ball and a flanker whose greatest asset was his speed and endurance in supporting his backs. In the face of a New Zealand public brought up on traditional All Black forward strength, that took tremendous courage. Most coaches would have seen where to go after the third Test. Gleeson spotted what to do instantly and, unlike England selectors who have tended to change too quickly without knowing just where they were going, he knew exactly the direction to go and brought in specific players to take him there. It was not so much a question of (for the sake of argument) Eveleigh not playing well, but rather that his style of play did not fit in with Gleeson's game plan. Mourie's did.

Most of us thought, after the second Test, that we were on our way to a victorious tour. Even a succession of hard games did not alter that feeling, the sort of games which led Moss Keane to coin the phrase: 'The first half was even, the second half was even worse.' (It was Moss, that splendid Irishman, with whom I roomed shortly after arriving in New Zealand. Just after five o'clock one morning he woke, noisily enough to wake me, scratched, and reached for his cigarettes and a can of beer. 'Bloody hell, Moss,' I said. 'It's five in the morning, bit early for beer and fags.' 'Sure,' said he, 'but it's five in the evening back home and I'd just be stopping off for a quick one on the way home from work.') We even had the luxury of a week's break from rugby, when we were dispatched north to the Bay of Islands, which is supposed to be semi-tropical. It rained. We cut our tour long-playing record there and it may be significant that the first song on it was entitled 'Lion Blue'. The itinerary then demanded that we make, not the short trip to Auckland for the Test match, but a trip all the way back to the far south of South Island to Dunedin, which was splendid management on someone's part.

Not that the twelve-hour trip had anything to do with our defeat in the third Test, by 19–7. We never recovered from a bad start, when Ian Kirkpatrick scored a try in the first minute, but the Lions forwards did well enough to feel afterwards that the game should have been won. I think the backs generally admitted that they had not, as a unit, been on top of their game. Defeat meant that we could not win the series but we could, at least, still share it. It was the least we deserved, even if we could not match the feat of the 1971 Lions in winning outright. All along we had suffered comparison with the 1971 party, comparisons which became more pointed when we were joined by several members of that side who were leading groups of supporters. Carwyn James, the coach on that tour, Barry John and Mervyn Davies – who might, if fate had been kinder to him, have captained the 1977 Lions – all joined the entourage, and they came at just the wrong time for our management who were, themselves, compared with the 1971 management of Doug Smith and James. The players never became neurotic about comparisons with 1971; many of us played with men from that party and accepted them for what they were, exceptional players. The management, though, struggling to build bricks without the same sort of straw, may have felt themselves to be playing the role of poor relations and naturally enough resented it. The 1971 party, after all, went out with everything to gain and it is to their eternal credit that they did so (remembering just for once that they lost the first game of their tour, in Australia); we left England with everything to lose, at a time when New Zealand had worked hard to redress the balance against them.

Even so, a share in the series was something tangible to return home with. We knew when we got to Auckland for the fourth Test that it would be hard so we gave our all. For seventy minutes we subjected New Zealand's forwards to all sorts of indignities, reducing them to a three-man scrum, such was the havoc we were wreaking on their ball. It was a travesty of our forward dominance that we should only have been 9–6 up going into the closing stages. Neary had come into the side because 'Cobs' was ill and he played superbly; Brown and Beaumont were outstanding and it took exceptional defence by the All Blacks to limit us to one try, scored by Dougie Morgan, who also converted it and kicked a penalty. Two penalties from Bevan Wilson kept the All Blacks in the game before I learned the hard way the lesson I have drummed into a succession of Leicester sides ever since. Always make sure that you find touch.

Phil Bennett fielded a New Zealand kick ahead near his own posts and I suspect his first thought was to open the game, just as he did in the classic Barbarians and All Blacks game at Cardiff in 1973, when Edwards scored what has been labelled the try of the century at the end of a 95-metre move. Phil's second thought was to find touch; he went for length and missed the line. Bill Osborne, the All Blacks centre, collected the ball and kicked back. Now it is worth noting that New Zealanders always chase high kicks whereas many times in Britain you see players ambling after the ball, thinking half the time that if they go hell for leather they will only have to walk back to the eventual line-out. In that respect New Zealand could be said to have created their own luck. They chase not in ones and twos, but threes and fours, so that when Steve Fenwick fielded Osborne's kick he could see the black tide bearing down.

I was alongside Steve and my first reaction was to drive in on him much the same as the forwards do on the catcher when the ball is kicked to restart a game and the tacklers are coming in. As I was coming in, Steve fed the ball to me when I had been expecting him to retain it and the misunderstanding was enough to have me off-balance as Mourie tackled me. The ball went loose and sat up for Laurie Knight to grab it and race to the corner for the try which gave New Zealand a 10–9 win – and the series. I have occupied the same sort of position in many other games, for club and country, because if you are able to read games correctly, you pick up the best place to be in defence. In some ways I had the same unfortunate experience in 1981 when England played Wales in Cardiff and I could see that Gareth Davies was going to kick for the corner. He did so, I caught it and passed inside for Dusty Hare to clear. Unfortunately he was caught, shovelled the ball away to Steve Smith who was robbed on the line, and Wales scored. That was bad enough but New Zealand in 1977 was heart-breaking, because of the complete injustice of it all. The whole sequence of events makes it seem as though we were doomed from the outset, though it may be fair to make another point on behalf of the All Blacks: in pressure situations they seem to control the ball much better than British players, and in speed of thought and reaction they are just that shade ahead. There was little chance of Knight knocking on that ball that bounced up round his knees – New Zealanders have been taking advantage of that kind of situation for years.

I still find it hard to regard that tour as a failure, even though the record books will describe it thus. It remains the second most successful Lions tour to New Zealand and I felt we came nearer to winning the series there than we did in South Africa in 1980. The pity of it was that it did not bring home to the British authorities the deterioration in back play – not that I think the 1971 backs would have found life easy in 1977. Defences are much more difficult to beat because the one thing that we have learned during the 1970s is that it needs no particular skill to organize yourself defensively on a rugby pitch. That knowledge is common to all rugby clubs; avenues of scoring have been closed – such as the front of the line-out from where I regularly used to score half a dozen tries a season – and it has become harder to open alternative avenues. I wonder if Barry John or Gerald Davies would have been able to operate in the same devastating way in 1981 as they did in 1971. To put it another way, if Mike Slemen or John Carleton had played in the 1971 Lions, their reputations would stand as high now as do those of John Bevan, Gerald Davies or David Duckham.

9

The Nearly Years

There is nothing like a Lions tour for experience, and not just of rugby. It seemed as though two years of living had been crammed into three and a half months, a concentrated period when most of us ran the whole emotional gamut from high to low, learned more about ourselves and our fellow human beings than we might have thought possible, and discovered how each member of the party reacted differently in conditions of stress. It may be that many people would hardly regard a rugby tour as stressful, comparatively speaking; all I can say is that they were not with us in New Zealand in 1977.

Not that we were finished with the tour yet when our aircraft took off from Auckland. After that fourth Test defeat the drinking and post-mortems went on long into the night and it was a bleary-eyed party that stumbled out at Suva where we were due to play one game against Fiji on the way home. But we had some stayers among us, notably on this occasion Fran Cotton, whose idea it was that eight of us sitting at the bar in our Suva Hotel should make it an all-night session, one of those splendidly spontaneous occasions where a group sits yarning, singing songs, recalling the good times and the bad. Fran, a man of considerable presence on and off the field, threatened anyone leaving the group round our table with dire retribution if they should sneak away during the night. 'There may be hundreds of islands in Fiji,' he said, 'and you can run but you can't hide – I'll find you.' Apart from Fran and me, there was Phil Bennett, Steve Fenwick, Clive Williams, Terry Cobner, Tony Neary and Chris Lander, rugby correspondent of the *Daily Mirror*. We sat out on the balcony overlooking Suva Bay and, as the night wore on, we each draped ourselves in a table-cloth to keep out the cold. The long-suffering barman would pop up every so often, saying hopefully: 'Last orders, gentlemen, before I close the bar.' The last time he said that was about eight o'clock in the morning.

As dawn broke Clive was dispatched for coconuts and we extemporized our own kava ceremony, accompanied by the traditional hand clapping. It is possible that the Fijians might not have recognized the ceremony which was followed by compulsory breakfast of greasy eggs and bacon, then syrup pancakes and a half of bitter, downed in one. Only rugby players could devise such a distressing ending to a memorable night and more than one of us suffered the inevitable consequences. We concluded with a swim in the hotel pool before attending the team meeting that morning – we were probably the first to arrive. It was just as well that we were not taking the game with Fiji too seriously. For us the serious business had ended the moment the final whistle blew at Auckland, so it is not entirely surprising that we lost to the Fijians, 25–21. Our preparations were low-key, the team meeting was held round the swimming pool immediately beforehand, but nevertheless we were in complete control of the game. Had it not been for the eccentricities of the local referee we would have won, but in a game when all the pressure in tight situations was on Fiji he insisted on awarding a stream of penalties to the home side. The balance at the end of the match was something in the order of two dozen penalty awards to Fiji and only two to the Lions which, added to the usual spirit with which the Fijians play the game, was enough to see them home. One penalty given against us came when our scrum was marching forward with the number eight holding the ball at his feet; it bobbed against the ankles of the second row and the referee gave him offside. It was that kind of farcical situation. Still, I dare say we boosted rugby considerably in Fiji.

By the time we reached Britain again it was mid-August and some three weeks later we were due to play a Barbarians XV in a match intended as rugby's contribution to the Queen's Silver Jubilee appeal fund. We were given details of the match on tour and we were told it would be treated like any other international, with the Lions gathering on the Thursday before the match. Had we been at home and contacted individually about the match arrangements I do not doubt that everyone would have acceded to them happily enough, but since we were all able to discuss the arrangements together we came to a communal decision that asking the players to give up another four days, just three weeks after returning to their families from a long, hard tour, was a bit much. Was it not possible, we inquired, to meet on the Friday and bring wives or girl-friends with us?

There was much wringing of hands from the organizing four home unions committee when the players questioned the ground rules for the game and, sad to say, I felt their eventual reaction was petty in the extreme. We realized the importance of the occasion and we all wanted to play in what would be a unique match, but equally we all felt that our families deserved more consideration. Since we had spent some fourteen weeks together playing rugby, it needed little more than some gentle organization the day before the game to prepare ourselves. We got our way in the end but only by foregoing the original accommodation in the London Hilton and retreating instead to the Star and Garter at Richmond. It was sad that we had to threaten not to play the game in order to achieve what we regarded as ordinary decent consideration, and sad that the organizers felt they had to maintain their authority by depriving us of a measure of comfort which we had seen all too rarely in New Zealand. It was not the first time, nor will it be the last, that rugby players were treated as recalcitrant schoolboys. The difference on this occasion was that the players were making their request from a position of strength – without us there would simply have been no game. The fact that all of us wanted to play, to prove that we were not as bad as we had been painted and to make a point against the famous players who had chosen not to make the tour, was neither here nor there. We had the satisfaction of winning 23–14 against a Barbarians side which included the French back row from their grand slam winning side, and Messrs J. P. R. Williams, Gerald Davies and Gareth Edwards, any one of whom, it was said at one time or another, might have made a difference to our tour.

Then, finally, the 1977 Lions were laid to rest and we turned to domestic matters. The seventies, it need hardly be said, had not been the happiest nor the most successful time for England in the international championship and the remaining years of the decade were notable as the 'nearly' years, when we achieved more than we had done pre-1977 but not as much as we might have done, given consistency of selection. England had many good players available but found difficulty in bringing them together, an opinion borne out by the remark made by Jean-Pierre Rives of France in 1980 when he said that the English pack worried him because, for once, all the Lions of England, scattered up and down the country, had been brought together.

I did not play against the American Eagles who made a short visit to England in 1977 for, like many other Lions, I took a long rest from the game. However, it came as no surprise to see one of the 1977 Lions – in this case, Billy Beaumont – being asked to lead the England XV which beat the Eagles comfortably at Twickenham. Roger Uttley had led England the previous season but it seemed obvious that a successor was being groomed in case his back injury prevented Uttley from playing. It did, as Billy led England into their first championship match, against France in Paris. We lost 15–6 to the grand-slam holders and felt mildly encouraged by the result in view of the circumstances: Andy Maxwell, the Headingley centre, went off during the game with a knee injury which ended his career; Peter Dixon, our experi-

enced flanker, went off at the same time with a sprung
collarbone. Having used both our replacements, Robin
Cowling dislocated his shoulder and almost fought Don
Gatherer when the England physiotherapist suggested
he should go off. Without him our scrum would have
gone to pieces. While he was there we held up, even if
under the greatest pressure. Robin stayed on, propping
with one good shoulder against Paparemborde. Several
times during the game the shoulder bone slipped out and
had to be replaced. I suppose if he had gone off straight
away he might have returned before the end of the season
but the damage he sustained made it a certainty that he
would not be able to play again that year. It was an act of
exceptional bravery.

We went on to lose our next game 9–6 to Wales at
Twickenham, a match in which the injury to Maxwell
allowed Paul Dodge to win his first cap. It may be an
English trait to derive comfort from defeat but, this
season, I felt it was justified. The Welsh team was loaded
with talented players but, on a dreadfully wet day, they
only won the match with a penalty after Bob Mordell,
England's flanker, got offside in front of his own posts. It
was Gareth Edwards's last game against England and he
left his mark, rolling us back time and again with those
immense touch finders. We were relieved to see the last
of him; it is difficult to take the broader view, that the
game was losing one of its greatest playing personalities,
when he had broken English hearts so often in the past.
English changes for the next game, against Scotland,
included the introduction of Maurice Colclough at lock
and the demotion of Mike Burton from tight-head prop.
Burton did not play again for England. On the one
occasion when I had played with him at tight-head and
Cotton at loose-head we had murdered our opposing
front row, yet the selectors insisted on regarding Fran as
a tight-head. When eventually Phil Blakeway came
along to play tight-head and Fran played loose-head we
won the grand slam. I do not pretend to know the
reasons why Mike could seldom win a regular place,

unless his disciplinary record and his joking attitude were held against him. But he was a hard man to best. He must have been utterly bemused the following season when England picked Barry Nelmes, a loose-head, to play tight-head and John Scott, a number eight, to play lock.

At all events we beat Scotland and won the final game, against Ireland, to move up to the halfway house in the table. It is worth pausing a moment merely to ponder the number of halfbacks who appeared in England colours that season and the following season. Against the Americans there was an experimental pairing of two northerners, David Carfoot and John Horton. Malcolm Young and Alan Old played against France before Old made way for Horton for the rest of the season. In 1978–79, Chris Gifford partnered Horton against Argentina, then Young replaced Gifford against New Zealand. Neil Bennett came in for Horton for the first championship match, then Young subsequently made way for Peter Kingston, the Gloucester scrum half. Lucky indeed is the country that has so many halfbacks of international or near international class. Unfortunately, not all of them were up to that standard and, even if they had been, they were not in the team long enough to prove it. It might have been said that the best of them, Old, was approaching the end of his career but he seemed to be doing very nicely for Yorkshire in 1983, so obviously his Indian summer is lasting longer than most – say, five years.

We had a cosmopolitan start to the 1978–79 season when the Argentinians played six matches in England and then were followed by New Zealand. Given that England had two 'warm-up' games before the championship you might have thought we would have made an impression on the international table, but you would have been wrong. We fielded a strong XV against Argentina at Twickenham and drew 13–13, a result which I believe surprised many people but which, put into perspective, only confirms the strides taken by Argentina in coming to terms with international compe-

127

tition. Then came the All Blacks, against whom many of us who had been in New Zealand the previous year were keen to do well. In any case, there is always a 'buzz' when New Zealand tour because so much is always expected of them. They are so good in aspects of the game where British sides are inadequate that they seldom leave without having taught us something. They had several newcomers and Graham Mourie, since his first appearance in the third Test against the Lions, had taken on a much more significant role as captain. He had obviously learned a great deal on the All Blacks tour to France in 1977 and, even though he had missed the home series with Australia in 1978, he had developed an excellent relationship with Jack Gleeson, the coach. That management team, of Russell Thomas, Gleeson and Mourie, got the utmost out of a party which, by All Black standards, was probably not exceptional. They had several close calls on tour but lost only once, to Munster, and became the first New Zealand side to win all four internationals here.

They did so because, like most New Zealand sides, they concentrated on what they were good at. Their support work was quite outstanding and they seldom tried any kind of move which was beyond their capabilities; and when you remember that when we left New Zealand in 1977 their tight forwards were in tatters, they had made vast progress on the road back to parity with British forwards. It may be that they were helped to such a successful tour by a lack of perception among British and Irish players, coaches and selectors – maybe in England we find some difficulty in distinguishing what the most successful features of our game are, and exploiting them until we build the confidence for more expansive play.

My first meeting with Mourie's All Blacks was at Leicester, where they beat the Midlands 20–15, the week before England's international with them. Dusty Hare kept the Midlands in the game with four penalties and a dropped goal and the All Blacks only made sure with

128

Front Rows I Have Known
Above: With Robin Cowling and Gary Pearce

Above: With Phil Blakeway and Colin Smart (just)

Below: *Left to right:* Graham Price, P.W. and Fran Cotton for the British Lions during the second Test, Christchurch, New Zealand, 1977

Above: With the boss, Ramon Howe, who says he likes to sponsor games at Leicester as it's the only chance he gets to see me!

Right: With Mum, not looking very happy about being dressed up

Below: The first front row with the wrong-shaped ball

Above: Margie introducing me to Ben and Tom in a rare moment at home

Below: The Monday golf crew − *left to right:* Andrew Gamble, Bernard Murphy, P.W., Leo McSwiney

Above: Robin Cowling trying to make up his mind whether to sidestep from his left or right foot

Right: Trying to hold off a couple of Wasps while waiting for Tim Barnwell to catch me up

Below: Gary Adey doing what he did better than anybody else

Above: Gary scored a few tries too — this one against Broughton Park in the John Player Cup, 1979

Below: Additional regalia for the Lord Mayor after the Town Hall reception following one of our John Player Cup wins

Above: Spot the difference. The old and the new John Player Cup

Below: Getting Fran Cotton into the position hundreds of props couldn't! Training in New Zealand, 1977

Above: Michelin-tyre man takes a ducking

Above: Watched by P.W., John Robbie and Andy Irvine, Clive Woodward shows Gary Player how he ought to be doing it

Below: The Suva night-hawks — a memorable all-night session in Fiji, 1977. *Right to left:* P.W., Terry Cobner (obscured), Fran Cotton, Chris Lander, Clive Williams, Phil Bennett, Tony Neary and Steve Fenwick

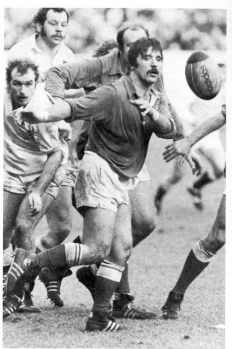

Above: Blood and black eyes for Jean-Pierre Rives (France) and Phil Blakeway (England)

Above: Robert Paparemborde (France). The most difficult of some very hard props to come out of France

Below: Philippe Dintrans (France). The charging bull and probably the best

Above: Two good mates, John Scott and Steve Smith, about to score from a move Budge Rogers said would never work

Above: Graham Price scoring for the Lions in the first Test against South Africa, 1980

Below: Bill Beaumont taming the 'Blue Bulls'. Lions v. Northern Transvaal, 1980

Above: Hong Kong Sevens winners — the 1981 Barbarians. Cheers! *Back row (left to right):* P.W., Brynmor Williams, Nick Preston, Gareth Williams, Andy Ripley; *front row:* Gary Pearce, Les Cusworth, Clive Woodward, Nigel Pomphrey

Below: Smithy and I could always force a smile

Above: England's court in session on tour in North America, 1982: key prosecution witness, Jim Syddall (right), has just shot down Les Cusworth's (standing left) alibi after cross-examination from prosecuting council John Scott (centre, with wings!)

Below: Syd Millar, Choet Visser, the South African tourists' best friend, myself and Willie John McBride on a tour I did make with him. Ellis Park, 1982

Above: The Lions pack before the last Test, South Africa 1980: John O'Driscoll, Graham Price, Bill Beaumont, P.W., Jeff Squire, Maurice Colclough, Clive Williams, Colm Tucker

Below: Midlands and North of England *v.* Argentina, 1976.
Back row (left to right): J. McVey, J. Moore, P. Hryschko, P. Dodge, M. Slemen, G. Adey, A. Bond, A. Neary, W. Beaumont, R. Trickey, I. Clayton, D. Forfar, C. White, H. White, M. Phillips, P. Lillington, J. Jee; *front row:* J. Carleton, S. Smith, J. Horton, P. Wheeler, F. Cotton, I. George, P. Knee, W. Hare, D. Cullen, J. Pearce. Eleven of these were in the Grand-Slam side four years later.

Above: The senior, some might say old, Lions as we liked to dress for dinner! South Africa, 1980. *Back row:* P.W., Graham Price, Derek Quinnell, Maurice Colclough, John O'Driscoll, Ray Gravell, Bruce Hay; *front row:* Jeff Squire, Syd Millar, Bill Beaumont, Noel Murphy

Below: Woody, Kobhead, the Bunch, Scoobie Doo and Brace before beating the French in Paris: Leicester's five internationals, 1982

Above: Paul Dodge, the players' choice as best centre in the world, ignored by two Lions selection committees, scoring against Ireland, 1981. Huw Davies backs him up!

Below: Top tourist Willie Duggan — the epitome of Irish character and spirit, with Sid Going bearing the brunt in 1977

Left: Chalkie White — the best coach by far that I have worked under

Below: Western Province President's team 1983. A great experience to tour and play with players from so many different countries. *Back row:* L. Cusworth, N. Youngs, J-B. Lafond, J. Murphy, J. Gallion; *third row:* M. Shaw, J. Perkins, R. Moriarty, G. Whetton, W. Duggan, J. Ashworth; *second row:* M. Ring, J-P. Lescarboura, D. Leslie, G. Knight, M. Slemen, R. Paparemborde; *seated:* B. Fraser, S. Wilson, I. Vodanovich (coach), P.W., S. Millar (manager), B. James, S. Pokere; *insets:* G. Davies and R. Bertranne

Left: Don't look at the girls! My last Test for the Lions, Pretoria, 1980

Below: Lions *v.* Northern Transvaal, 1980: getting rid of ball to John Robbie (9) before Northern get rid of me

Below: I always said I would remain cool and emotionless if I scored a try for the Lions: Timaru, 1977

their third try, scored by Mark Taylor late in the game from what I can only describe as an unfortunate long throw over a line-out by the Midlands hooker, who shall be nameless. Four of us played again at Twickenham seven days later when, in the absence of the injured Cotton, the selectors asked Barry Nelmes to move across the front row to tight-head and moved Scott to lock. It was the sort of experiment which they might just have toyed with against the Americans; to do it against the All Blacks was asking for trouble and we got it. We lost 16–6 and, if fortune had favoured the All Blacks, they might have doubled their score.

It was the sort of failure which laid us wide open to the 'first game, first loss, all change' syndrome to which English selectors are prone. Not that change was not needed, in view of the original selection. Out went Scott, out went Nelmes, out too went Dixon, Hare and Horton. There are so few opportunities during an international season to prove yourself that any side starting on the wrong foot finds itself constantly rebuilding, unless the selectors retain a degree of faith in their original choice, given the necessary breaking-in period. They did not have that faith and we never recovered. A good start against Scotland was wasted when we could only draw 7–7 at Twickenham. We lost to Ireland and were lucky to beat France 7–6 at Twickenham, a game in which England were under a lot of pressure but tackled grimly against a French side which did not always do itself justice. France themselves had just beaten Wales by a point, which was sufficient justification for some of England's supporters to suggest we had a prospect of beating Wales at Cardiff. Sometimes I cringe when I look back at some of the idiotic comments made regarding the Welsh match by people who should know better. The Welsh team was said to be their weakest for ten years, England had beaten France (smashed them by a point), and our prospects were said to be good. How many countries can claim to go to Cardiff as favourites to win? Even the All Blacks admit they have to overcome the fervent atmosphere and would certainly not admit to being favourites, even though recent history suggests they have become so.

Suffice it to say that we lost at Cardiff 27–3, the worst defeat since 1905. Sometimes I feel we have not progressed very much since then. We just managed to avoid the wooden spoon and the season marked the end of Peter Colston's reign as coach and that of Sandy Sanders as chairman of selectors. Peter was a very pleasant man but needed to be more dogmatic, more positive in his approach. Before the game against France that season, in fact, he did lay things on the line and the team responded, but it was far too late. He worked well with the players and he had plenty of useful ideas. In different circumstances he might well have flourished, and there is always a lurking suspicion that the coach may not have had his way in obtaining the players he wanted. He was succeeded by Mike Davis while Sandy's job went to Budge Rogers, with whom I had toured in the Far East eight years earlier. Budge had hardly stopped playing for Bedford before he became a selector and now here we were again, on another tour to the Far East in the early summer of 1979 but this time with Budge as manager and me as a senior player.

The tour, the first by England for four years, gave the new management team the chance to shake out some of the cobwebs left over from the previous season and allowed the players to assess their new coach. We knew Mike mainly as a hard-working lock from the 1960s and a successful coach with the England schoolboys. As far as we at Leicester were concerned he had been given the job ahead of our own club coach, Chalkie White, whose track record was second to none. Inevitably we were biased in Chalkie's favour but it was hard to ignore the fact that Mike had no senior track record at all. Nevertheless I tried hard to keep an open mind; I assumed that if he had been made coach ahead of Chalkie then he must have some very special qualities. For his part, I suspect Mike regarded Leicester players with a degree of wariness, knowing that we had prospered under Chalkie's direction and that all the time we would be comparing the approaches of the two men.

In his first year Mike showed himself to be slightly naive in dealing with senior players. By the end of his second year I felt that he had adjusted and had become a good international coach. Initially he approached the job using the same terminology he had used with the schoolboys and treating the three-week visit to Japan, Fiji and Tonga as though it were a prolonged training session for the next international championship. In fact, you cannot relate such a tour to the mud and cold of Twickenham or Cardiff eight months later. The use of such short tours – apart of course from the contact with an International Board country that they bring to the hosts – is for the squad to get to know each other and their coach and thus to develop mutual trust and respect. But you cannot ignore the tour schedule, ignore what must be done to beat Japan, or Fiji or Tonga. As it happened we received something of a shock in the first game against Japan, when we won only 21–19 at Osaka, a conversion by Hare making the difference right at the end.

Mike learned from that. The day before the game we had been doing sidestepping exercises, forwards too; we had been doing basic things like practising rucks, or 'whooshes' as Mike called them. Suddenly senior English forwards found that, instead of practising mauls, we were doing 'clutch-accelerator' exercises; this may have been fine for schoolboys, expressing exactly what Mike wanted from basic game situations, but it was unnecessary for senior players. What we needed to be doing was preparing to impose our superior physique on the Japanese, dragging them into mauls, using our greater upper-body strength – they were probably better at sidestepping than we could ever be, anyway. But Mike was not pig-headed; indeed his greatest attribute in that first year was his willingness to listen, to modify his own views, to understand what a clutch of former England captains like Neary, Cotton and Uttley had to say. Gradually his training sessions developed a style of their own though I could never rid myself of the feeling that if he had gone from the schools to a senior club such as Bristol, put in three years with them, the slogging matches with Gloucester, the midweek evening hauls down into Wales, and built up his experience of the current senior game, he would have gone into the England job with his confidence considerably enhanced.

Nevertheless we were all happy to try to put his ideas into practice and we emerged from that tour with seven wins out of seven. Among those victories was the 19–7 win over Fiji, when I had the impression that our hosts were being forced to modify their natural carefree approach to the game in the cause of better results. Their officials were obviously seeking higher standards and regular contact with the major rugby countries and, with this end in mind, they asked Arthur Jennings, the Fijian-born New Zealand lock of the late 1960s, to coach them, hoping to improve their major weakness at the set pieces. They were taught to discipline themselves and this was foreign to their whole way of life; their rugby, full of rush, gush and high spirits, reflected their existence and now this was being sacrificed on the altar of efficiency. The players themselves seemed unhappy at being asked to curb their desire to run the ball all over the place. Though they have a comparatively large playing population of 11,000, it is scattered throughout some 300 Pacific islands which have too few administrators and not enough money to take them as far afield as they need to go.

They have done tremendously well to have progressed as far as they have but I do not believe they should lose their individuality in order to progress further. I know that since they came to Britain in the sixties and early seventies and caught us on the hop, other countries have learned how to play against them, to keep the ball tight and tie them down at rucks and mauls. Nevertheless, the Fijians should build on what they do best, their formid-

132

able athleticism and running ability. A greater degree of organization on the field does not mean that they also have to evolve a new style of play which they do not enjoy. This is the great pleasure which travel in the world of rugby brings: the chance to see different nations stamping their own characteristics on the game. Just imagine how boring it would be if all countries found themselves playing the same way. I appreciate that the Fijians believe greater success will bring greater recognition and enhanced prestige, but is the sacrifice of their natural game worth it? From the events of their unhappy tour in Britain in 1982, I would doubt it.

10

Season in the Sun

Whatever virtues are possessed by an out-of-season tour, continuity is not one of them. Players become used to adopting the methods of one coach, then return to their own clubs where they may be required to adopt different methods. Several months later they meet once more for the first international squad session of the season and find themselves picking up half-forgotten threads. It appeared to many of us that 1979–80 would be just such a season, of picking up the threads. We all hoped for the best, as you do at the start of any international season, but the visit of the All Blacks gave us reason to ponder the difficulties which might lie ahead. It was New Zealand's third tour to Europe in three years but there were only eleven survivors from the party which, a year before, had won all four internationals. In the build-up to the game against England they had contrasting fortunes against the country's two most successful rugby-playing areas, wiping out the Midlands 33–7 at Leicester in the fourth match of the tour but crashing 21–9 to a quite outstanding Northern Division XV at Otley one week before coming to Twickenham.

The Midlands side which I captained was based, once again, on the Leicester club and we were quite clear in our approach – we would move the ball wide and try to get round the All Blacks cover on the wings. Our plan fell down because we did not have a back row quick enough to win the ball when we were stopped. We did not, in short, have a Mourie. The New Zealanders had one other important motivating factor in their favour about which we could do nothing: the day before the game the news had reached them that their coach of the previous season, Jack Gleeson, had died of cancer. All of them knew Jack, liked and respected him, as I did myself from the little contact I had had with him, and all of them wanted to take the opportunity of a last tribute to him and his style of rugby. They got off their coach and strode into the ground with a concentrated look in their eyes, knowing just what they had to do. They scored five tries against us and even if the match had not taken on such emotional overtones, we would probably still have lost.

In games such as this, of course, it helps to have had some pre-match practice, but since the abolition of the divisional championship we were denied that. So it was greatly to the North's credit that they should have developed such a successful game plan. You could draw a direct parallel between their game and the one played by the combined North and Midlands against the Argentinians three years earlier. Both sides embarked on the match with specific ends in mind and stuck to them. The North, at Otley, played a kicking fly half in Alan Old, they developed driving forward play close to the rucks and mauls and they had Tony Bond playing the game of his life in the centre, knocking down the All Blacks midfield and still fast enough to get in for two tries. It was a total triumph and was ignored by England to the extent that they chose Rafter on one flank instead of Uttley and, more importantly, Les Cusworth at fly half rather than Old. The international itself, which we lost to New Zealand 10–9, lingers in my memory only for the fact that at one time it looked likely to be Les's one and only cap. He was brought in to form a new halfback pairing with Steve Smith and asked to do a job which Old had done superbly the week before but which was not Les's natural game. He had not even been on the Far East tour earlier in the year, as he should have been. Maybe England thought they could beat New Zealand playing a running game, hence the selection of Les and

135

Richmond's Nick Preston at centre. The overall plan was not entirely clear to the players but if we were aiming at an ambitious game, we needed first to have developed the confidence which only comes from winning. At the other end of the season, with three wins under our belts, we achieved this against Scotland; New Zealand as the first game of the season was a different kettle of fish.

It was disappointing, particularly for the players from the North, but at least the senior players and Mike Davis had established some kind of dialogue. Mike welcomed contributions from Billy, Fran and Nero. It was not a question of players taking over sessions but a sensible discussion of the overall tactical approach as opposed to blind faith in the coach's ideas. It is not a teacher–pupil relationship between coach and players at international level, more a matter of coordination to ensure that the players are all operating towards the same end. Before the international championship began, the selectors had a flash of inspiration. I have never been shy of criticizing selectors but they must be given credit for pulling Phil Blakeway out of the ruck of the final trial and making him tight-head prop for the first game, against Ireland. 'Blakers' had come on the scene several years before, much heralded by Gloucester: 'You think Burton and Cowling were tough,' they told us. 'Wait until you see this lad.' Then he broke his neck and it took several years before he filtered back into the top-class ranks. When he played for the Rest in England's trial, which both Fran and I missed through injury, he wrecked the England front row and destroyed Clint McGregor's chances of a cap. Fran was moved over to loose-head as it was recognized that, as the Lions selectors three years before had indicated, he could play quite happily at loose-head as well as tight-head, and Phil came in to show almost immediately that he was the same class as Cotton and Price.

That was a major contribution towards the grand slam. The front row was as solid as I had ever seen it. The second row would have been Billy Beaumont and

136

Maurice Colclough but Maurice was injured and Nigel Horton, late of Moseley and by now playing in France, came in. Nigel was a hard, experienced player who did not always receive the most gracious treatment from the selectors – nor did he this season for, after playing well against the Irish, he was dropped and Maurice was restored. Uttley and Neary joined forces with Scott in the back row; John Scott had matured as an international number eight and he had two of the most experienced and effective flankers in the game alongside him. No one could complain about the forwards; the selection committee, who could boast little playing experience as tight forwards among them, had done well.

Behind the scrum John Horton was restored at fly half instead of Les Cusworth. That was bad luck for Les but, in view of the original selection for the New Zealand game, not entirely unexpected. Indeed, there seemed no reason why Old should not have been chosen for that specific game against the All Blacks. Sophisticated selection can involve a 'horses for courses' situation, where you pick particular players from your squad depending upon who will provide the opposition in the next match. It was important to know that Steve Smith was firmly ensconced in the scrum-half seat. He has always been a tactically aware player and could be depended upon to work well with Neary and Uttley, his fellow northerners, driving off the side of rucks and mauls, making sure that when the backs were given the ball it was good ball. The centres were a good mix of solidity and pace, in Bond and Preston, and the wings, Slemen and Carleton, were two of the best in the four home countries. Behind us all was Dusty, whose first cap had been way back in 1974, against Wales. If there was one player who could not have been adequately replaced that season, it was he. In every other position there was a viable alternative but not at fullback – since Dusty won his first cap England had given games to Peter Rossborough, Tony Jorden, Alastair Hignell and David Caplan, but none of them kicked goals like Dusty did or gave such breadth to the attack. I will admit he is not the perfect fullback – opposing fly halves would hope to stretch him about the field and sometimes he has shown a weakness under the high ball, but his attributes far outweigh his faults. How many times has he been discarded, only for the selectors eventually to return to him? Lesser players might have thrown in the towel and opted to play no more for their country but Dusty has kept plugging away, doing what he does better than many another fullback, scoring points. Andy Ripley was another player who had obvious strengths to his game as a number eight, but certain weaknesses. By harnessing the right combination of talents in the back row, Andy's strengths could have been exploited and his faults hidden. Dusty had two very dependable wings to help him in the defensive chores which allowed him to concentrate on his primary function, goal-kicking.

England were lucky too, that season, to begin at home against Ireland. Not that Ireland were anyone's pushover – they had done well on tour in Australia the previous summer and were well fancied themselves for the championship. They had discovered a goal-kicking phenomenon of their own called Ollie Campbell and they had an experienced pack. But they did not have the same charisma as that developed by Wales and France during the seventies and their forwards found themselves totally absorbed in trying to hold a rampant English pack. In doing so they conceded tries to Smith, Scott and Slemen, all of them converted by Hare who also kicked a couple of penalties. We won 24–9 and the only blow we suffered came when Bond, who had been having such a good season, broke his leg and was replaced by Clive Woodward. Clive retained his place for the visit to France for the next match while Colclough returned to the second row instead of Horton, who had played his last game for England.

At last we were achieving some stability. In contrast the grand-slam pack which had served France so well was breaking up. Bastiat and Skrela had gone, Imbernon

138

was injured and Palmié suspended. They had a good front row, which included Paparemborde and Dintrans, but the fear that Rives had of the English pack was justified. It was the most controlled forward display I have ever experienced in an England jersey and we won in France for the first time in sixteen years, by 17–13. But it was never easy. France led to begin with and rallied strongly at the end and the whole match was clearly going to be decided on any aspect of play in which one side or the other could exert a dominating influence. That area was the English pack. Preston and Carleton scored tries, Hare kicked a penalty and John Horton kicked two valuable dropped goals while Uttley was off the field receiving attention for a head injury. It was a big match for us and confidence soared in the knowledge that, this season, Wales had to come to us.

We had to make a further change before the Welsh game at Twickenham, because Preston, an original selection for the match, cried off injured and Dodge joined Woodward in the centre. We were all sufficiently experienced by now not to take anything about the Welsh for granted. Too many of us had suffered for that in the past. But the press went berserk about the match. All the old grudges came home to roost during the fortnight between our win at the Parc des Princes and 16 February 1980. The Welsh too had beaten France in a rugged match which was followed by a variety of accusations of rough play. Price, it was suggested, constantly collapsed scrums in a dangerous fashion. He, not unnaturally, responded to the criticism and the players, on both sides, could hardly avoid being swept along on the tide of recrimination. Everywhere you turned the game between England and Wales was being discussed. Even if you stopped reading the papers, you could not stop friends and colleagues at work from pointing out this, that and the other likely feature of the forthcoming match.

I had never before appreciated the meaning of the phrase 'you could cut the atmosphere with a knife', but I sensed what it meant at Twickenham on the day of the match. The expectancy among the crowd was overpowering. People were on the edge of their seats, waiting for something to happen. They were not to be disappointed, for Paul Ringer, the Llanelli flanker, was sent off by David Burnett, the referee, after fourteen minutes for a late tackle on John Horton. I had felt before the game that the appointment of Burnett was the wrong one for this particular game, although it is fair to say that the appointment was made before circumstances attached so much extra significance to it. Burnett is a good referee and has developed into a first-class international official but, for that game at that time, I believe he was the wrong choice. It was only his third game and I had seen an instance of his pre-match nerves before his first international, Wales v. England in 1977. Of course he was nervous before his first big game, we all are, and I had tried to bring some light relief by producing a pair of golf shoes from my kitbag when he came round to inspect the studs. I thought it might provoke a smile and allow him to relax but by the look on his face when he saw them, spikes and all, it seemed he was too wound up to appreciate the joke. Since that time he had refereed only one further international and it appeared to me that someone with more experience was needed, someone like Norman Sanson, the Scot, for whom players everywhere had considerable respect, someone who would not be intimidated by the atmosphere.

It was a brave action on Burnett's part to send Ringer off – it was, after all, only the second time a player had been sent off at Twickenham in an international match – but most of the players were aware that, having made his gesture, it was unlikely he would do it again and so the dismissal had little effect on an already aggressive game. It may sound extraordinary, in view of all the subsequent publicity, but I was not aware of the extent of the foul play in the game. It was hard and committed, but then so are most internationals, and it came as a surprise to read the fiery criticism in the papers the next day and to see afterwards the film of various incidents in the game. The one incident I do recall was lying trapped at the bottom of a ruck and seeing one Welsh forward coming towards me. He was a man with whom I had toured several times and while I did not expect him to walk round me, I was surprised when he looked down at me, stamped on my head, and was off. Looked at another way, and without intending to make light of what was not a funny situation, I suppose you could say that if we had not been friends on tour together, who knows what he might have done.

Ringer's dismissal changed the course of the whole game. The heady atmosphere at the start was heightened when Wales were placed with their backs to the wall and responded, as so often a side does when they lose a player, by raising their game. They knew what a famous victory it would be to beat England at Twickenham with fourteen men and in my view they were unlucky not to do so. Given better goal-kicking they must have won, for though they scored the two tries of the match, through Jeff Squire and Elgan Rees, neither was converted and several penalty chances were missed. Their atrocious kicking underlines the point about Dusty; he kicked three penalties, the third in injury-time, which won the match for us 9–8.

Ringer did no damage to Horton in the late tackle which caused his dismissal, though that may have been more by luck than judgement. I had seen both sides of Paul Ringer when he played two seasons for Leicester between 1973 and 1975. He had been a good friend of mine and was popular among the players, though not perhaps with the committee. He was a skilful, aggressive, sometimes ruthless footballer and there were occasions when he went over the top. He lacked an element of self-control which makes a great player yet in many respects he could be described as a good influence on other players in the team. Yet, away from the field, he was a delight to be with. He would roll up to the club in his battered old Morris 1000 with a shotgun and his fishing

141

tackle in the back seat. That justified him calling it his 'sports' car. It had no discernible brakes and Paul claimed there was no reverse gear on it either. After matches he would sing in the bar. He had a splendid voice and always insisted on complete quiet when he was performing. When he left Leicester we were all delighted to see him re-emerge with Ebbw Vale and win his Welsh cap before moving on to Llanelli.

After the game at Twickenham I sought him out while the official dinner was still going on and found him at one of the hotel bars with Derek Quinnell, his club colleague. Both of us wanted to console him but his only thought was that he had let his team and his country down. I do not think he was too worried about what rugby's hierarchy would think. All he was concerned about was that, had he stayed on, Wales might have won. He played once more for Wales before signing professional forms and joining Cardiff Blue Dragons in the Rugby League.

This England–Wales match itself was a watershed. It indicated that the game had reached a stage where physical confrontation could go beyond acceptable bounds. It served as a warning to everyone, in what happened before and during the game. Playing for your country is emotionally stimulating enough without the media sensationalizing the game; it is an important occasion but only in comparative terms and within fixed limits. To make it out to be more than that is to do the game a disservice. It may also be of some significance that some years had elapsed between the last Lions tour and that game. Looking through the seventies there were comparatively few dirty games involving the four home countries. The regularity of Lions tours and the increasing availability of lesser tours means that players from England, Scotland, Ireland and Wales have the chance to get to know each other much better than before, to respect each other. But it had been three years since the Lions toured and so newcomers had emerged on the international scene, some of whom may not have had the chance to establish relationships with many players from different countries. A not dissimilar incident occurred in 1977, again three years after one Lions tour and immediately before another, when Geoff Wheel and Willie Duggan were sent off for fighting during the Wales–Ireland game of that season. Not that, in my own case, a friendly relationship had prevented that Welshman from stamping on my head!

I am not a great believer in luck when it comes to winning or losing games of rugby but over the course of a four-stage race it would be difficult to erase all trace of good fortune. England used all that was going for them against Wales and, having won that match, we were through the thickest part of the wood. Already it was our season, there was no doubt of that. Victories over France and Wales were so rare as to be cherished and we then had a month to ponder the last hurdle, against Scotland at Murrayfield. There was no danger of complacency setting in; we had an extra training session at Stourbridge and those of us who had battled away on England's behalf for several seasons without any reward were certain that we were not going to let our chance slip now. Our approach to the Calcutta Cup match was very cool, very professional. We were like workmen preparing for a specific job, checking that all the tools were in working order. There was little sign of nerves and this became obvious during the first half of the game in which our tactics were as clinically effective as they had been against France.

There was one scrum at Murrayfield which I regard as the best I have ever been part of. It took place near Scotland's line, our own ball, and Billy called for a double-shove. The ball was heeled, the scrum locked and pushed and I can still recall the feeling as we surged forward, like a super-charged car going into overdrive. The only way to stop us from scoring a pushover try was for Scotland to collapse the scrum which their lock, Alan Tomes, attempted to do by buckling inwards. That in itself was risky since he would have been trodden underfoot but Steve Smith finally released the ball and put Carleton in for a blind-side try. The sensation from that scrum was an uncommon experience at international level. Occasionally it happens at the end of a club game but you do not expect that sort of surge against an international pack at an early stage of the game. We led 16–0 after half an hour, through two tries by Carleton and óne by Slemen, and 19–3 at half-time, Hare kicking a penalty to go with two conversions. We were so far ahead that we became slightly loose in the second half and Scotland, to their credit, came back strongly. But our points cushion was always too much for them and two more tries, from Smith and Carleton, with a second penalty from Hare, gave us a 30–18 win. It must have been a tremendous game to watch. I saw the edited highlights later on television which were a source of considerable pleasure.

The feeling after winning the grand slam, triple crown, championship – all the prizes denied to England for so long – is difficult to describe. There was elation, yes, but overall there was a sense of relief: relief that we had done the job we set out to do, relief that all the hard work and preparation had paid off, and relief that players like Neary (whose forty-third and last international it turned out to be), Uttley and Cotton had finally participated in the domestic game's richest reward. The four Leicester players who had contributed to the grand slam, Hare, Dodge, Woodward and I, had travelled to Edinburgh together by train and we returned home the same way, but this time in one of the train's coaches chartered by a Leicester travel agent and crammed full of England supporters. Many of them were wearing grand-slam jerseys which had been manufactured even before the match and we were a festive crew as we travelled south, hardly thinking that, behind us, the Lions selectors were choosing the party to tour South Africa in the summer.

In 1977, when Wales won the triple crown but were denied the championship by France, there were sixteen Welshmen in the original tour party to New Zealand.

How many Englishmen, then, deserved to go as Lions in 1980 after winning the grand slam? As it turned out, only eight, the front five forwards, the two wings and a centre. Even allowing for the unavailability of Neary and Uttley it seemed a poor reward, though there was no doubting that Billy would get the captaincy, the first Englishman to lead the Lions since Doug Prentice in 1930. The party was: Bruce Hay, Rodney O'Donnell, John Carleton, Elgan Rees, Mike Slemen, Peter Morgan, Ray Gravell, Jim Renwick, David Richards, Clive Woodward, Ollie Campbell, Gareth Davies, Terry Holmes, Colin Patterson, Phil Blakeway, Graham Price, Peter Wheeler, Alan Phillips, Fran Cótton, Clive Williams, Billy Beaumont, Maurice Colclough, Alan Tomes, Alan Martin, Derek Quinnell, Stuart Lane, John O'Driscoll, Jeff Squire, John Beattie, Colm Tucker. These were joined at various intervals by Andy Irvine, Paul Dodge, Tony Ward, John Robbie, Steve Smith, Gareth Williams, Ian Stephens and Phil Orr, which meant the addition of two more Englishmen to the original number.

I think perhaps the genuinely unlucky ones were Dodge and Scott, who had both played really well during the season. As it was, Dodge came out as a replacement and immediately was picked for the third Test, which suggests that someone made an initial mistake. As things turned out, neither Hay nor O'Donnell had the happiest of tours and I suspect that, if Dusty had been chosen, he too would have ended in the Test side. It would have been very enjoyable too to watch him kicking in the thin air of the Transvaal, if only to see how far he could propel the ball. The other player we desperately needed was Neary, who felt that he could not spare the time from his business. The lack of pace in our back row was cruelly exposed when we lost Lane in the first match of the tour and it was a deficit which, despite the many and varied talents of the other back-row players, we could never make up.

11

Rugby in Black and White

I had no qualms about going to South Africa. I had received a letter from an anti-apartheid organization asking me to consider turning the tour down on moral grounds, as did many of the other players, but I did not believe that all sporting links should be broken. The arguments for and against playing sport in South Africa have been rehearsed time and again and it remains incredibly difficult to know on which side to come down.

It is important to remember, in the context with which we are dealing, that to be a British Lion is the ultimate honour for players from the four home countries. It is the end towards which all internationals work and to contemplate rejecting the chance to be a Lion is almost unthinkable. Most of us are inclined to think of the extent to which the situation in South Africa directly affects us, as individuals, which is nil. It is also obvious that if you do not go yourself, there will be half a dozen other players willing and eager to take your place. So whatever gesture you make will have no practical effect. There is the other side of the coin to be considered too. If I, as an English rugby player, refuse to go I deny myself the chance to get my view across to South Africans – players, administrators, any members of the public I happen to meet; I lose the opportunity to try to convince South Africans face to face of the need to keep changing, and to tell them that whatever progress they have made so far must be continued and improved upon so that they do not become more and more cut off from the rest of the world.

Politicians have always been quick to seize upon sport as an easy target. It costs nothing, unlike the severance of trade links, and it attracts a great deal of publicity. They can be seen to be doing the 'right' thing. The Leicester club suffered from the bombast of local politicians after four of us accepted invitations, as individuals, to visit South Africa in 1982 as part of the team to help celebrate the reopening of the Ellis Park Stadium in Johannesburg. The Labour-controlled city council, who are Leicester's landlords, passed a resolution saying they would have no contact with anyone who could be linked with South Africa. There was some talk about how they might be able to punish the club for the actions of a very few of its members and the council chairman refused to attend the Lord Mayor's reception for the team after the 1983 John Player Cup final.

My answer is to ask whether the council make the same strict scrutiny of the dealings of all their commercial tenants. How many of them are linked in some way with South Africa? Have the council bothered to find out, and if they have positive proof of links with South Africa, would they then refuse to rent property or ground space to such firms? It is all too easy to make political capital out of sport. In any case, where do you start drawing your moral lines? You can talk about Russian invasions of Afghanistan, of South American dictatorships, or you can talk (just for the sake of argument) about the local council at Bedford who might have decided to reduce services for old people or to decrease the money spent on local hospital development. Because you disagree with their actions, do you then contemplate not playing Bedford at rugby? Very few rugby players, after being picked for a tour abroad, sprint to their gazetteers to check on the politics of the country to which they are going. They go there conscious of no barriers, to play rugby and to talk rugby, and the difference in ideologies is irrelevant. I appreciate that not all members of the black and coloured races in South Africa may be impressed when an Errol Tobias or a Hennie Shields reaches the top in the white man's sport. The majority of them are more interested in reaching the top in a world which is neither black nor white, but surely if players from both worlds are competing together, talking together, appreciating each other as people, it must do something, however small, to break down the apartheid system.

While we were there the players had little serious discussion of apartheid. We could not ignore the fact that it existed – it was brought home to us by the notices indicating separate facilities for the various racial groups. On the other hand we were staying at large international hotels where guests were both black and white and the situation seemed entirely normal. Most of the hotel staff were black and we would laugh and joke with them, pull their legs as any team on tour does, regardless of the colour of the men and women looking after them. It was difficult therefore to meet black or coloured people on an equal footing so I deliberately set out to obtain permission to visit one of the black townships, to see for myself what sort of conditions existed there. I achieved this when I met a man in Durban who was director of a charity established to help the population on the township some fifteen miles outside Durban. The charity received money from industry and used it to introduce better living facilities for the blacks and to foster better relations between the racial groups.

The director obtained the necessary government permission and showed me the township himself. The contrast with the city of Durban, modern and sophisticated in the Western sense of the word, was horrific. Here were tens of thousands of people living in the most primitive conditions, in shacks made out of wood, out of corrugated iron, in some cases out of cardboard boxes. The local river was too badly polluted to use for drinking and water tankers brought in supplies, which meant long queues of people waiting in the hot sun with whatever utensils they could manage. Set in the countryside as

148

they are, there is plenty of room for development in these townships and projects exist to provide better homes, even to try to tailor such homes (within limits) to the requirements of the individuals who will live in them. Such projects only scratch the surface of the problem at present and my guide was keen to see sweeping change come as soon as possible.

We did, of course, have plenty of opportunity to talk to whites about their country and found two distinct groups. On the high veldt, in Transvaal, in cities like Johannesburg, Pretoria and Bloemfontein, there were the Afrikaners, most of them hard-line nationalists who would be prepared, literally, to fight to the death rather than allow the blacks and coloureds equality. Talking to them I came to understand some of the history involved – how the ancestors of the Afrikaners came to South Africa from Holland in the seventeenth century, how they began settling the country before many of the black tribes came down from the north, how they regard themselves as the rightful heirs to the country, if only on a first-come basis. They are a very religious people. Many Springbok sportsmen do not drink or smoke because their religion forbids it and quite a few are, or become, lay preachers in their church. There is a strong belief in the family unit yet, for all this, they hold quite rigidly to the view that apartheid is right. This was something I could not begin to understand, a strong belief in the family of God existing side by side with an equally strong belief in the separate development of the various racial groups.

Coming down from the veldt we encountered the more liberal views expressed in the coastal areas, many of them by people of British descent. There was a belief that change was long overdue. Such people could see the injustice of the system and were feeling their way towards a solution but they felt that change had to come gradually, not in two or three years but in fifteen or twenty. They had seen what happened in other African countries which left the British Commonwealth to claim

149

a gleeful independence, only for their new rulers to run the economy into the ground or for dictatorships to become the norm. Integration, the liberals believed, was a slow process which allowed the black and the coloured races all the rights and privileges enjoyed by whites but only after they had learned to use and appreciate them. Children should be filtered into the educational system so that they could learn the art of government and administration. Many of them were sufficiently realistic to know that the world would probably not allow them the time they felt was needed to achieve their goal.

I came back from South Africa generally satisfied that the average white South African admitted the need for change but that the Afrikaners would, by their intransigent attitude, delay the problems from being resolved. As far as the sporting organizations were concerned, I had the impression that they could not go much further along the road to integration. Cricket has taken immense strides, football is the black man's game anyway and the South African Rugby Board claim there is no apartheid in their game – and dispatched a multi-racial side to Britain in the autumn of 1979 to prove it. What happens in practice, as far as rugby is concerned, is that the blacks go to the black clubs and the whites to the white clubs (as a general rule) in the same way that Welshmen and Scots in London gravitate towards London Welsh and London Scottish. It is like calling to like. Some of the better black players join predominantly white clubs because they are that much more ambitious and seek higher standards. But the main point which cannot be avoided is that, however many changes are made in sport, the laws of the country remain unchanged. Sports clubs may work on a multi-racial basis, but outside the individual clubs the system remains unchanged. Since that tour I have tried to keep track of what is happening in South Africa but there seem to have been few legislative changes which suggest that apartheid as it affects life in general is decreasing.

There was also some rugby, inbetween the injuries,

but though we lost the series 3–1, as the Lions did in New Zealand three years before, it was a thoroughly enjoyable tour. It is difficult not to enjoy South Africa even though, in strict rugby terms, a tour to New Zealand ranks slightly higher on the scale. There was not the sense of claustrophobia we felt so often in New Zealand; the weather is warmer, there are so many different places to see, and so great a variety of entertainment is laid on. It may be unfair to compare conditions there with the abnormally wet winter we endured in New Zealand but it is inevitable.

Even so, some of the eventual frustrations were the same – worse in some ways because, even allowing for the unprecedented run of injuries which necessitated eight replacements, the Lions could still have won the series. All the Tests were close, with the possible exception of the second at Bloemfontein when the Springboks sprinted clear with two late tries after leading for most of the match. Even then we lost Gareth Davies at a crucial stage, but the first and the third Tests, lost by four and two points respectively, could have been won had we exercised just an ounce more control. We won the fourth Test and even though there were only four points between us, the feeling among the forwards was that we smashed them.

South Africa undoubtedly learned from their uncomfortable experience in 1974 when the Lions roared through their country without losing a single game. Throughout that Test series they dabbled with selection, making mistake after mistake, and they were determined not to do it again. They made their experiments before the 1980 Lions arrived, by inviting a South American team to tour and playing two internationals against them. There were six changes in the Springbok team that played South America in the first international and the Springboks who played the Lions at Cape Town in the first Test and, among them, was the discovery of a superb counter-attacking fullback, Gysie Pienaar, from the Orange Free State. Despite their limited oppor-

151

tunities at international level I felt the standard of rugby played at provincial level in South Africa remained high. There were many talented players to choose from and it was largely a matter of bringing the right combination together. The South Africans were quick to see that the Lions were short of pace in the back row after Lane was injured and that it would help their cause to move the ball wide, away from the main source of Lions strength, knowing that big flankers like Rob Louw and Theuns Stofberg would be pounding up in support. It is no coincidence that Louw scored tries in the first two Tests and that Stofberg scored in the second Test and played a vital role in the decisive Springbok try in the third Test.

On the Lions side the management were conscious of the need to impress ourselves physically on the South Africans and we worked hard on our forward play. The front five were unchanged throughout the Test series but any attempt to develop a style of play behind the scrum was thwarted by a succession of injuries to the halfbacks. There was genuine quality among the halves, Terry Holmes and Colin Patterson at scrum half and Gareth Davies and Ollie Campbell at fly half. Only one of them, Campbell, finished the tour and he had not been available for many of the early games because of a hamstring injury. In the fourth Test we had John Robbie at scrum half and Steve Smith as replacement scrum half, neither of whom were original selections. Gareth damaged his collarbone in the first match, Ollie strained a hamstring in training, Terry hurt his shoulder and was finished off by a damaged knee, and Colin, who lasted longer than anyone, received a knee injury in the penultimate game which was so severe that he did not play first-class rugby again.

In those circumstances it was difficult for the backs to cultivate a pattern of play though I did not believe the forwards consciously retained possession because of that. After the tour ended we were criticized for over-use of the rolling maul but, at the time, it was a feature of British play which was successful and against which the Springboks had to develop an effective answer. Technically we were better among the forwards though it would be wrong to say we dominated South Africa in the same way we had against New Zealand in 1977. We won all our provincial games so there was no shortage of confidence among the players, which was reflected perhaps in the way we rallied from 16–6 down in the first Test. We went ahead 19–16, then when the Springboks scored a converted try we got back to 22–22 before Divan Serfontein, their scrum half, got the winning try.

That game stands out in my mind for two reasons: Tony Ward's goal-kicking was amazing, for he scored five penalty goals and a dropped goal. His kicking out of hand was deplorable, for he missed touch on several occasions which gave South Africa possession they had not earned. They promptly ran the ball back at us. When we should have been tying the game up we presented them with the ball; it was a painful lesson to go with the one I had learned in unhappy circumstances during the closing stages of the fourth Test against New Zealand: find touch. When we lost the second Test too, then our best prospect was to share the series and at 10–6 up in the third Test at Port Elizabeth and ten minutes remaining, we looked as though we were on the way. That was when Clive Woodward, in an unaccustomed position on the wing, sidefooted a kick ahead gently into touch, Germishuys leaped a low fence, grabbed the ball and threw in to Stofberg, then took the return pass for the try while the rest of the players were still struggling to reach the scene. The conversion gave South Africa the game, 12–10, and the series.

The situation seemed unreal. We felt we were playing well enough yet there we were, three-nil down and the series gone because of lapses of concentration, no more. If we had won by a couple of points rather than lost by a couple, those lapses would hardly have come under the detailed scrutiny they subsequently received. Sometimes I think that there are players who do not realize that some action of theirs may have contributed towards an

153

opposition score, because that score is not an immediate one.

All the Lions had left now was the last Test. On any tour you begin by aiming for a clean sweep, to win all four Tests. If that objective becomes unattainable then your target is modified, but a target has to remain and all we had to aim at was this last opportunity in Pretoria to prove ourselves, to recoup some lost pride. It was unthinkable, after all the hard work we had put in and the pleasure we had had in each other's company, and despite the number of players who had been forced out of the tour by injury or (in the case of Fran Cotton) by illness, that we should return to Britain without at least one win with which to console ourselves. Poor Fran. We had some great times together, for England and on tour, and South Africa in 1980 was no exception. On one occasion we were hacking our way down a golf course in four-balls and I was playing with Clive, David Richards and Gareth Davies. I missed a green and when I went to chip back I found my ball nestling next to a snake. I retreated hurriedly before my caddie told me the snake was dead. When we had all holed out I gingerly picked up the snake and popped it into the hole for the next four-ball to discover. As it happened it was Fran who first putted successfully and went gleefully to reclaim his ball, only to find the unwelcome 'guest' I had left him.

The build-up to that last game could not be compared for intensity with the atmosphere in Christchurch before the second Test with the All Blacks. It resembled more nearly the last leg of England's grand slam, when all the players knew exactly what could be achieved and how we would go about it, the feeling that one task remained uncompleted before we packed up and went home. Having beaten Western Province 37–6 in the last Saturday game before the fourth Test, we knew we were still playing well and it may be that the Springboks, having the series in the bag, relaxed slightly.

We won 17–13, the first time the Lions had won the last Test of a series in South Africa since the Second

World War, but even then we could not resist making life difficult for ourselves. We were only 7–3 up at half-time, after a penalty by Campbell and a try by Clive Williams, and we were winning so much ball we should have been out of sight. Worse was to come in the second half when Willie du Plessis scored a try and Pienaar kicked two penalties to give South Africa a 13–7 lead. But it all came right by the end, when Andy Irvine and John O'Driscoll each scored a try and Campbell kicked a conversion. The result gave us at least a degree of satisfaction and I think we all returned home happy in the knowledge that there was little more that each of us, as individuals, could have done to affect the outcome of the tour.

In the light of all I have said concerning South Africa, it would be hypocritical to suggest that England should not go to South Africa in 1984, as they are scheduled to do. But there is no doubt at all that the Rugby Union are faced with a most unenviable decision because the ramifications are so wide. They have to consider the likely consequences for other sports, in particular the Commonwealth Games to be held in Edinburgh in 1986 or indeed the Olympic Games in Los Angeles in 1984. If those games became affected by a boycott from the black countries, then the hard work of so many athletes would go for nothing because the high level of competition they seek in the games would be lost. On the other hand there is an overwhelming urge to resist the political blackmail which the threat of boycott implies. Rugby has to have the resolve to do what it considers right. I also have to remember that it is easy to stand back and be judicial. I have been fortunate enough to go to South Africa on several occasions; had I not yet gone, I would want to have the opportunity at all costs because international players always want to pit themselves against the best the world has to offer, and some of the world's best players are in South Africa. Nor do I, as an individual, have to make a decision which could affect the sporting careers of many other people outside my own sport.

There is another important element in the discussion.

What road will South Africa take if England rejects her now? In the last five years Scotland, Wales and France have been unwilling or unable to tour South Africa. Australia are not allowed to tour there and the New Zealand government is keen that no All Black party should visit the republic. If England too turn their back on South Africa, what use is that highly prized place on the International Board to her? Danie Craven, president of the South African Rugby Board, places great store on his links with England and he is a strong enough personality to carry his country into a situation of independence from the International Board. We encountered Dr Craven several times in South Africa, notably after the first Test in 1980 when several of us, myself included, walked out during his speech at the post-match reception. We felt on that occasion that he was using the Lions to make political capital before a large assembly of the world's press and television. He told his audience of the great strides forward being made in South Africa and I felt the truth was being embellished in order to create the impression that the country as a whole was changing. That having been said, I am in no doubt that Dr Craven has done his best to create multi-racial rugby in his country. If, after that, England tell him they will not tour, it will be the ultimate affront because England – whatever the merits of their playing record – remain a focal point for world rugby, as in so many other sports, because of the part they played historically in originating or administering the game. Then South Africa may look in other directions for support and could become a focus for emerging rugby nations who may feel that they are not receiving sufficient recognition from the established countries. To tour or not to tour – that is the question.

12

Picking and Choosing

Some people never get enough of a good thing. In the summer of 1980 I was something of a glutton because, three weeks after the Lions return from South Africa, Leicester made their first overseas tour in celebration of their centenary season. We had six matches organized, in Australia and Fiji, and I had attended to many of the arrangements. Then I found I might not be able to play on the club's tour, the penalty of some horseplay in our hotel in South Africa the night following our fourth Test win. A cushion fight had developed in the foyer and I was caught from behind by an unexpected blow delivered by a member of the medical profession. The cushion jolted my head to one side and I heard several clicks in my neck. The next day I was very sore and the flight home was made in some discomfort, my embarrassed assailant administering to me in a manner more suited to a personal assistant than a busy doctor.

Despite all the traction I had on my neck back in Leicester it was obvious the injury would not have cleared up before the club tour but the officials kindly said they would take another hooker, at considerable additional expense, and I went after all. I did play in the last game of the tour, against a Fijian President's XV, partly because my travel contact at the Fiji end pressed me to do so and partly to justify my being in the party, but I was relieved to come through unscathed. The injury, I should emphasize, had nothing to do with the neck injury I had suffered in my second international five years earlier nor was it that injury which prevented me from playing for Leicester in their game against the Romanians, who were completing their tour of Ireland in England. I required an operation to remove a small stone from my foot and therefore missed the rare opportunity of being on the wrong end of a 39–7 thrashing as Romania proceeded to put us in our place.

All was well when the 1981 international season came round, with England going in as champions – but not with their grand-slam side. It had taken the best part of seven years to get that side together and it lasted for just one season. An injury in December dictated Neary's retirement and Uttley came to the conclusion that he too would have to give up after more back trouble. Cotton made a remarkable recovery from the illness which had hit him in South Africa and received clearance to play, but his condition forced him to leave the field during the first international, against Wales at Cardiff, and sadly we saw him no more on a first-class rugby field. That was three substantial props gone from the side and although we could bring in the reliable Mike Rafter on the flank, another prop was knocked away when Hare was dropped unnecessarily halfway through the season. He scored all nineteen points against Wales and eleven more against Scotland but was judged to have been at fault in both matches when the opposition scored. In addition, lightning struck twice: when Cotton, the loose-head, went off in the game against Wales he could only be replaced by a specialist tight-head prop, Austin Sheppard, and the scrum was not so comfortable. Then against Ireland we lost Phil Blakeway, playing at tight-head, through injury and only had a loose-head prop available as a replacement – his Gloucester colleague, Gordon Sargent. Even so we came through against Ireland but it was not the luckiest of seasons.

The game against Wales, which we lost finally 21–19, represented the best chance we ever had of winning at Cardiff during my career with England. Indeed we were winning 19–18 going into injury-time before Brynmor Williams dummied a pass from the base of the Welsh scrum, Woodward put a foot offside and Steve Fenwick kicked the penalty. Another penalty in the last few seconds gave Hare the chance to kick his way into the history books, as he had done at Twickenham the year before, but this time he could not make it.

I do not believe there is any bogey in the minds of English players about the international at Cardiff, despite the fact that we have not won there since 1963. We all know there is very rarely any such thing as a weak Welsh team. Equally, most countries hope to do better at home, with their own spectators cheering them on, and most countries reserve their best for England, who are the old enemy in whatever sport you care to choose. We have so many skeletons rattling around in our cupboard, hangovers from an imperial past when the English lorded it over all and sundry. There is great respect for Welsh club players in England, though it is probably fair to say, unhappily, that the reverse is not true. I do not believe the Welsh respect the game as it is played in England, though they may think well of certain sections of the game and certain individuals within it. There are few English clubs who go into Wales and win. The exceptions generally are the western clubs, Gloucester, Bristol and Bath, while Moseley took on a lot of Welsh fixtures some years ago and did well. The Welsh will look at our club results in the Sunday papers, they will see our games on *Rugby Special* and they will recognize a different and lesser, standard of play from the one they are accustomed to. England are supposed to have over forty first-class clubs while Wales have no more than a dozen of consistently high standard. Geography has given them what England have lacked hitherto, a concentration of good players at a handful of clubs; but means of travel have improved to such an extent that we in England really should be capable of organizing ourselves to offset our geographical problems.

Even the Welsh would have enjoyed watching Woodward score a marvellous try in the 23–17 win over Scotland at Twickenham. The lead changed hands five

159

times during the game and we came to realize the sort of effect that Jim Telfer's coaching was having on Scotland. No longer could we rely on beating them, as we had come to do for the last five years – which coincided with the time Gordon Brown stopped playing for his country. The Scottish forwards were much tighter and we really knew we had been in a match. The same was true in Ireland, but despite our difficulties in the front row we won and went into the final game against France at Twickenham hopeful of a share in the championship. Those hopes blew away down the wings of a howling gale, with which France played in the first half and scored sixteen points, including the famous try which should never have been awarded, stemming as it did from a quick throw-in at a line-out with the wrong ball. Many of the England players did not appreciate that the original match ball, which was kicked into the crowd, had not been used and so it did not affect our game in any way. Marcus Rose kicked four penalties but we lost 16–12. Even so, considering the various disruptions we had suffered that season, we had not gone too far back, a feeling that was confirmed by some resolute displays on tour that summer in Argentina.

That was one tour which I had to miss. I had been present when Margaret gave birth to our first son, Ben, in December 1979 and I was keen to be there for the birth of our second child, which turned out to be another son, Tom. I had been away nearly all the previous summer and there had been few years before that when the close season had been kept genuinely free. Any player is reluctant to turn down a tour with his national side and this was the first occasion when England awarded caps for games against non-International Board countries, but it was time for a break. Quite apart from our domestic situation I had captained Leicester for three years, including our hectic centenary season, and I have already outlined how time-consuming a job club captaincy is. I decided to see Tom into the world and save myself for the Australians.

Australia arrived in the autumn of 1981 hailed as world champions, which was a title not of their own seeking but was awarded by the press after they had beaten New Zealand (who had beaten South Africa, who had beaten the Lions). We knew quite a lot about the Australians at Leicester. We had played the Queensland state side, who had been coached by the Australian coach, Bob Templeton, the previous year, and we had played three of their leading sides on tour. And it was at Leicester that the Australians were to begin their tour, against a Midland Counties XV containing seven Leicester players. Chalkie White hit the nail on the head after we had watched videos of Australia's games against New Zealand: 'Think of the doubt going through their minds,' he said. 'They've never played well on tour in Britain, they are not used to our conditions, they've got a lot of young lads in the party and this is the first game of their tour.' Suddenly all the doubts I remembered at the start of the Lions tour to South Africa came back: how would I cope with the hard grounds, the heat, the glare of the sun? It must have been much the same for the Australians coming to the mud and cold of a British autumn. We made a good start to the game, put points on the board, and the Australians found that they could not retrieve their position. From my place as hooker, watching at the front of a line-out, I could see the confidence evaporating, the heads going down, and we won 16–10. The tour itinerary did them no favours either by putting them in against the North in their third game (which they drew 6–6), Bridgend in their fourth (lost 12–9) and Wales B in their fifth (won 10–9).

I played against those Australians three times – it would have been four but for the cancellation of the Barbarians game – and I felt their forwards were better than they were made out to be. They needed a vital edge in confidence which always seemed to be denied them. It remains a matter for conjecture how their tour might have gone had they won their first game and conquered the strange conditions and their opponents at the earliest opportunity. They returned to Leicester for the twelfth game of the tour, fresh from their only international win, over Ireland. This time however they won 18–15, which was annoying from the club's point of view because we led 15–12 with five minutes to go. Hare kicked two penalties and two dropped goals and Cusworth a third dropped goal before Paul McLean kicked a long penalty which staggered over the bar and brought them level. Then we were penalized again for a bout of fisticuffs and the Australians pumped a long ball down into our corner. From the line-out Mark Ella dropped the goal which won them the match. However, when it came to the international it was quite a different story, England winning 15–11. There were severe distractions at half-time during the game, provided on the one hand by the naked charms of Miss Erica Roe and on the other by someone dressed as a gorilla who climbed onto the pitch. None of the players noticed the 'gorilla' except Colclough who said to me in the bath after the game: 'You know, I was amazed how the boys' attention wandered in the middle of an international, just because some guy gets on pretending to be a gorilla.' Poor Maurice had not noticed Miss Roe streaking across the pitch.

The forwards played well against Australia, and Maurice was outstanding – he had kept his mind on his job anyway. All seemed to be well as we went into the international championship but we stumbled at the first hurdle, provided by Scotland at Murrayfield. We were already well aware that they would be no soft touch – Wales discovered that too at the other end of the season – but we were leading 9–6 deep into injury-time when Colin Smart barged into Iain Paxton and Irvine kicked the equalizing penalty from his own half of the field. It was a silly way to throw away a championship point but at least we had Ireland at home in the next match before the fates started to rock our boat. Maurice had been hurt against Scotland and though he was fit to play against Ireland, he had not played any rugby inbetween the two games and he looked a bit rusty. Then Billy Beaumont suffered a head injury in the county championship final and was forced to drop out. We did not appreciate at the time that he had played his last game for England. Steve Smith was appointed captain, Jim Syddall came in for Billy and then, two days before the game, Paul Dodge dropped out with a hamstring injury, which meant a return for Tony Bond. The Irish, as it were, caught us with our trousers down, slightly disorganized fore and aft, and took their chances well to win 16–15. One of their tries came from the ginger-headed prop, Gerry McLoughlin, to which Ollie Campbell added a quite magnificent conversion. I doubt if he had much more than a yard to aim at, across the wind from near touch, but in the end his success made the difference between defeat and victory; and if ever a kick deserved to win a game, that one did.

I had my own problems going into that game. In training at Stourbridge the Monday before the game we had worked hard in scrummaging and by the time I got to bed that night I could hardly move for a pain in my back. Ironically enough, if I had been asked to succeed Billy in captaining England, I do not think I could have coped with it that week because my only concern was being fit enough to play. Extra responsibility would have been entirely beyond me. I went to see Terry Moule, the naturopath osteopath who did so much to help Roger Uttley with treatment for his damaged back. I virtually moved in with him for two days, receiving constant treatment, until on the Thursday I was in a position to tell the selectors that, if they could excuse me from the Thursday training, I should be fit by the Friday. It was Terry rather than I who believed that and he was right. I survived a rigorous fitness test and, by the eleventh hour, the morning of the match, I was at last convinced I could play.

Inbetween the Irish game and the match with France we learned that Billy's withdrawal from the game was permanent. He had developed into a magnificent forward and an equally capable captain. There was no question but that we would miss him, not just that season but for the next two or three years when England might have hoped to use his talent and experience. To offset this major disappointment there was a natural pride in Leicester when Dodge was restored to the centre with Woodward, Hare returned (after being only third choice when the international season began, behind Rose and Nick Stringer), and Cusworth came in at fly half. Five players from one club was a quite outstanding achievement. In France, Mike Davis took me aside for a quiet word on the captaincy. Nothing had been said before, when Steve was appointed against Ireland, and Mike explained that the selectors felt his boisterous good humour would give the side a lift against the Irish to counter Billy's absence. Having made that step, it was felt that to derive him of the captaincy in Billy's continued absence would make him appear a scapegoat for the defeat at Twickenham. From remarks that have been made since then it appears that Mike would not have been averse to having me captain the side, if not that season, then the following season.

Against France we badly wanted to put our game together, as a tribute to Billy if nothing else, who was there in his new role as television commentator. The French contributed to our chances by picking two number eights in the second row and a lock at prop, we won enough ball to set up positions for Hare to kick nineteen points and we won 27–15. It was a superb game and we let off steam accordingly in the evening – perhaps too much steam. It was more like a volcano. We had the usual journey from the Parc des Princes into the centre of Paris for the post-match banquet and England's players were seated at two separate tables. As is the custom at French games there were little gifts at each man's place; sometimes it takes the form of a record, or a cigarette lighter or after-shave. On this occasion there was a bottle of after-shave for each player and, sitting with Maurice Colclough, I saw him empty the perfume from the bottle and refill it with white wine. Strange, I thought, until

164

Maurice stood up and shouted: 'After-shave!' There had been contests between the two tables all evening, of course, as so often happens, and this was just one more challenge. Maurice whipped the top off his after-shave bottle and drank the contents off. When Colin Smart, at the other table, rose in response and repeated the feat I thought: 'He's in the joke too.' But an hour later Colin complained of feeling unwell. He must have been taken in by Maurice's drinking 'feat' and he was taken, post haste, to hospital leaving chaotic scenes behind him. The English committeemen were shooting black looks at the players, who by now had napkins knotted round their heads and trousers rolled up to the knee, aping the traditional Englishman abroad. One of the problems was that in Paris the visiting teams tend to drink wine in the same way as they normally drink beer, by the potful; the bread rolls were flying around and things gradually deteriorated.

The upshot was a letter from the chairman of selectors to each of the players warning them about their be-haviour on future occasions while representing England; though there was an additional irony in that the only change to the squad for the game against Wales brought Stringer in as replacement fullback for Rose, who was the only teetotaller in Paris. I was vaguely aware of having played a part in the horseplay and, before Budge's letters to the England squad arrived, I wrote to David Brooks, president of the Rugby Union, and to his opposite number in France, Albert Ferrasse, apologizing for any untoward behaviour. I received an understanding letter from the French president which said, in effect, that 'garçons will be garçons'.

Horseplay and 'wrecking' have come to be accepted as part of the average rugby player's behaviour over the years but we should always be careful that the wrecking remains a private affair, rather than spilling over and affecting any third parties. What is described as high spirits in a rugby player is called hooliganism by the world at large and there is no reason why players should be treated any differently from other people. When my rugby career began, tour parties or away teams would usually rely on one or two older individuals staying sober and keeping an eye on any behaviour that got out of hand. Any damage was generally paid for by a whip round among the players the following morning or by the club secretary writing a cheque so as to ensure that the team had somewhere to stay on tour the following year. Nowadays people are inclined to accept no excuses for outrageous behaviour and to call the police. As in anything there are degrees of anti-social behaviour and if it can be kept within the bounds of a private room, a blind eye will be turned to much of it. When it affects outsiders, who have nothing to do with rugby, then it becomes unacceptable. The only mitigation that can be put forward is that rarely, if ever, do players act maliciously; but that may not be much comfort to a hotel proprietor gazing upon the battlefield of his hotel after the warring tribes have departed. Players will have to remember that an appearance in court is a possible consequence of 'high spirits' in the eighties.

The hangovers had cleared by the time the Welsh came to Twickenham, where we gained a most satisfactory 17–7 win, and then it was time to depart to Canada and the United States for a tremendously enjoyable tour. We did not go there just to throw the ball around and entertain the locals. We went to develop our rugby the way we wanted and we played well doing just that. We were accompanied not only by Budge Rogers and Mike Davis as the tour management, but by David Brooks and the president-elect of the Rugby Union, John Smith, and most of us got on well with the alickadoos. Few of us would have believed things could turn so sour for England during the 1982–83 season.

There is seldom any one reason you can isolate when a side suffers a fall from grace as England did that season, from being championship favourites to wooden spoonists. Perhaps in the first place we were over-valued for our performances on tour, when in eight games we scored 352 points and conceded only thirty-four, and similarly the sixty points we scored against Fiji and the forty-seven against the Rest in England's trial match contributed towards a misleading impression. Perhaps we were slightly over-confident about reproducing similar form in the championship itself. But the season had started off on the wrong foot – literally – with the boot-money scandal. Manufacturers in this country had to submit details of payments made to players for wearing their brand of boots to the Inland Revenue and they wrote to the players concerned informing them of the circumstances. The four home unions became aware of this and, of course, had to take action since the rules relating to amateurism in the game were plainly being broken.

It was the Rugby Union's reaction which instantly created a 'them and us' situation between players and administrators. They assumed that all the leading players had taken money and their initial decision was that any markings on boots worn by players representing England, or at important games at Twickenham, should be blacked out. Meanwhile they continued to hold meetings in an attempt to get evidence implicating individuals when, quite plainly, they were never going to get the proof they wanted. No player was going to tell them and be automatically suspended from playing; the Inland Revenue are obliged to keep their affairs confidential and the boot manufacturers, Adidas, were not going to play Judas. The common-sense attitude, and that adopted by Wales, Scotland and Ireland, was to acknowledge that payments had been made and either to ignore it or to establish a situation in which no payments would be necessary, by taking out a contract with a specific firm of manufacturers to supply the Rugby Union with equipment, as Wales did in July 1983.

In the end the Rugby Union opted for the latter course but by that time it was too late. We, the players, had all been branded as criminals and any feeling of mutual trust which had been established over the years was

167

dissipated. Even Phil Crowe, captain of Oxford University that season, found himself and his team tarred with the same brush when both sides were asked to black out boot markings before the Varsity Match and he not unnaturally was very displeased. So we arrived at the farcical situation where, before a major representative occasion, England players were sitting in the Twickenham dressing room fiddling with felt-tip pens when they should have been concentrating their minds on the match ahead. Of rugby's officialdom it was the selectors who were closest to the players and I feel sure they should have voiced the players' feelings strongly to the Rugby Union, just as Willie John McBride did when he declared that if the four home unions wanted his Lions to worry about boot markings, they would have to find themselves a new manager.

The players have no direct voice on the Rugby Union's executive committee so they have to rely on the selectors to create for them the best atmosphere in which to prepare for matches. Many of us felt that the actions of the Rugby Union indicated that the selectors had aligned themselves with the officials. Of course the Rugby Union had to be seen to be taking some kind of action but that did not give them an excuse to brand every player coming into the England squad as a potential or actual law-breaker. They should have made the best of a bad business by taking a firm decision straight away which, if it involved a contract with an equipment company, would have had the additional advantage of bringing substantial funds into the game in general. Instead they dallied and sowed the seeds of discord. It was not as though the situation was truly unknown to them before autumn 1982; rumours of payments to players have abounded for years and they did not have to wait for the Inland Revenue to prod them into acknowledging commercial interest in the game and taking advantage of it.

Into this rather unhappy atmosphere dropped Mike Slemen. Or rather, he dropped out of it, because he was ignored for the trial despite having been on England's

168

left wing for twenty-nine games. Already we knew we would be without Blakeway (through retirement), and here was another seasoned player of proven world class whom we seemed likely to be deprived of. We had not been disturbed when he was omitted from the Fiji game because that was the sort of game in which newcomers can be tested. But now he was not even a replacement for the trial and, worse still, received no kind of official explanation of why he was dropped. It created a feeling of tremendous insecurity and the reasons which were eventually given in the papers for his demotion were unconvincing. People I met in Leicester, members of the public who had seen Mike play, seemed as taken aback as the players were, and I told one selector of this when he was chatting about the reaction to the trial sides. I was told it was felt Mike had not played well the previous international season and that his current form was not sufficiently good to keep out aspirants to his place.

That disagreed with what players from Lancashire were saying. According to them, Mike was not quite as sharp as he had been but you must remember that the more experienced internationals tend to pace themselves through the early part of the season in the hope of reaching a peak for the international matches. In any case there were no aspirants to his position because, in the trial teams, two right wings had been chosen on the left, Tony Swift and Barry Evans. In the end Tony played three games on the left and was then dropped in favour of another right wing, David Trick, who did not know he was playing on the left until the decision was made in Dublin during training, two days before the game with Ireland. We, players and selectors, were supposed to be part of a team pulling together to beat the other four countries and the only inference the players could draw from the whole episode was that the relationship we had thought we had with the selectors either did not exist or was unimportant. I had thought we had progressed from the fifties and sixties, when players may not have expected to be given explanations for their non-selection. After all, in any well-run club, players are told why they are picked and why they are dropped, and while accepting that the situation with national selection is somewhat different I would have thought any player who had established himself internationally and given years of service to England was entitled to know the reason why he is eventually dropped.

When Woodward dropped out of the French match with the lingering effects of a shoulder operation, we had lost three world-class players. We lost a fourth when Colclough played only half the French match but, nevertheless, England still went down to Wales and achieved a better result than any other team for twenty years. The 13–13 draw may have been in some respects disappointing but the players did not think so as they trooped off the field at Cardiff. Certainly Steve Smith was not dejected and when Budge went into the dressing room and told him to stay with the players while he (Budge) handled the post-match press conference, Steve agreed. Then we learned from the papers that Budge had castigated the halfbacks for throwing the game away – not the forwards as a unit or the backs as a unit but specifically the halves – and this only half an hour after the game when emotions were still running high.

I had felt all season that Budge was looking for an excuse to get Nigel Melville into the team and that chance had now come. Nigel is a talented player and will undoubtedly serve England for many years but Steve was the man in possession and had done nothing to deserve being dropped. He had played well, he had taken over the captaincy at a difficult time, he had led a successful tour in America and he had played half a game against Wales with a cracked rib. But out he went and out went the fly half, Les Cusworth. In came Nigel and then out he went again, unable to win his first cap against Scotland because of an ankle injury. (Incidentally, how unlucky can one individual be? In the space of five months Nigel lost the chance of an England cap and then of a Lions cap when he became a replacement in

170

New Zealand, only to be injured when his form suggested that a place in the Test side was open to him.) Into the side for the Calcutta Cup match came, not Nick Youngs, the designated replacement, but Steve. The players were confused and concerned at the way the selectors seemed to be messing the side about. It came as no surprise to hear during the close season that Mike Davis told a coaching conference that he had not been able to have his way on three specific issues during England's season, and that he regretted not having pressed harder for them. One wonders to what extent the whims of individual selectors put England's prospects at risk.

Having criticized selectors to my heart's content, I feel obliged to give some indication of what I look for in a selection panel. First of all, let me discount the theory that players may try to hide a poor performance by passing the blame to the selectors for not doing their job. No one can stop players questioning selectors' decisions – it would be an odd player indeed who did not pause to think why England, in the middle of the 1982–83 championship season, decided on a major change of emphasis by dropping both their halfbacks. They would not query the introduction of the newcomers; they would look at it the other way round and ask why the former occupants, in this case Smith and Cusworth, had been dropped when they had done nothing obviously wrong. Once the side has been chosen, however, the players accept it because to go into a game wondering why a certain individual was picked would be fatal.

The problem may lie not so much in the realm of selection itself but more in that of communication. Selectors need not necessarily feel obliged to open their hearts on every adjustment they make to a side but they should be expected to offer some explanation on major policy decisions, to indicate, for instance, what they expected from Nigel Melville and John Horton that Smith and Cusworth had not provided. When a squad of players has been through a tour, a representative game, a trial and two internationals together and then finds two of their number dumped right out of the squad, it is reasonable to expect a degree of explanation, if only to show that the selectors are clear in their own minds about their aims and objectives. So often in the past there has been that sneaking feeling that change has been made for change's sake, in the vague hope that things will get better rather than for any logical reason. Something very drastic must be supposed to have happened if, on any given Saturday morning of an international, a player is worth his place, yet by the evening he is not. The selection process should be thorough enough to provide a substantial reason for any player to be picked for his country in the first place. If that player is a new cap, then he needs more than one or two games before he can begin to stamp a definite impression on the game at international level.

If, of course, selectors are doing their job properly, you seldom hear about them, unless with a flash of inspiration they pick a Blakeway out of a ruck of players and discover their prayers have been answered. I do not believe in large selection panels, at any level, though I doubt if you could get away with a rugby 'supremo'. Any union who gave the authority for selection into the hands of one individual would have to be terribly sure they had chosen the individual correctly, although any selection panel, however large or small, is always accountable to their union's committee.

The coach to the national side should have considerable weight attached to his views. He, after all, is the man who has to prepare the side and if he wants specific players to carry out his game plan, he should be given them. I suspect that, under the present system, the coach finds himself overruled too frequently for his own comfort. However hard a coach may fight to get the players he needs, he may not be able to convince the other selectors, and the larger the panel, the harder the coach's job will be to make sure every member appreciates what he is trying to do.

In an ideal world I would like to see some kind of management person – give him what title you will, chairman of selectors, team manager, coordinator, convenor, whatever – whose job is to attend to the peripheral organization of the team, to liaise between them and the union executive committee, between players and hotel managers when on tour or abroad, and generally to ensure that the atmosphere surrounding the team is as good as it can be. He could also hold the casting vote on selection on a panel which contained a senior coach and an assistant coach. The senior coach would look after the overall tactical direction of the team and, if he was a forward, his assistant should be a back, so that each major team unit had specialist preparation. If the assistant was better in delivering team talks, that responsibility could also be delegated to him without the senior coach losing any authority. There would thus be a natural channel of progression when the time came for the senior coach to step down.

In essence, this is what happens on tour where selection is carried out by the team manager, the coach and the team captain. There is no reason why a three-man panel should not do the job at home though the team captain would not be expected to have a vote. He may, in an era of stable captaincy, expect to be consulted over certain issues as I am sure Billy Beaumont was during his twenty-one games as England captain. Indeed, there were times when selectors consulted me as a senior player, though how much notice they took of my views I was never altogether certain.

Selection itself is a gathering-in and sifting of information from a variety of sources. You do not have to award a vote to people in order to hear their views on the players with whom they have much more contact than a national selector can manage. You very quickly discover whose views are worth respecting and whose views to treat with a pinch of salt. England now have four divisional technical administrators ideally placed to pass on judgements of players' performance. There is an

173

under-23 coach, the senior club coaches, the schools coaches at the sixteen and eighteen-year levels, all of them intensely involved in the game. Together they create a network all over the country, and you can go even further in your search for information; if, for example, you hear of a young Bristol player worthy of consideration, there is no reason not to ask his club captain about him, if that captain is an experienced and respected senior international such as Mike Rafter. Although Mike would be keen to advance players from his own club (just as senior club coaches would be) he would never be so foolish as to push forward a player who would quickly be seen as failing to make the grade.

The press can be treated in the same way. There are journalists whose views are generally respected and those you ignore. I have heard selectors say they never read the papers. I do not believe that for a moment but if it were true, it would be a foolish attitude. Journalists are continually watching players and talking to players, coaches and administrators up and down the country, assimilating opinions. That is their job and, in consequence, they probably know many players much better than selectors do, so what they say in print may well provide selectors with a pointer which they can then check out through other sources. There is certainly no need to dismiss the press out of hand.

The Welsh selectors have shown that they can spot potential internationals at an earlier age than their English counterparts but then their club system helps them to do that. If a young player goes on making breaks in Welsh club rugby without someone finding a way of restraining him, the chances are that he is a good player. In England the seventies were littered with the names of players who won one or two caps and then disappeared from the international scene because the system lends itself to the flash-in-the-pan performance. A player may look good in a county championship semi-final or final but the chances are that the following week he will be back playing against second-grade opponents without

174

having proved that he is consistently capable of performing well.

Sometimes selectors do not seem to appreciate how great a degree of specialization there is in 1980s rugby. We had, in 1978, the situation where a loose-head prop was picked at tight-head for England and a number eight at lock, which was a howler of the worst kind. The situation at prop is generally accepted now just as the difference between open and blind-side flankers has been accepted for years. But a lock is no longer just a plain lock either: he packs on the left or the right-hand side of the scrum and jumps at two or four in the line-out, and there is a difference in the duties of the two positions. If you are on tour and are selecting from a limited party then a degree of versatility is useful, but if you have an entire country to choose from you surely go for the best player in his individual position. It must raise the overall team standard if you have a specialist in every position. The same is true for left and right wings. Their lines of running and their areas of defence are different and it is not so easy as selectors seem to think merely to change them round and expect them to operate with equal efficiency. At international level a player needs to be operating at 100 per cent efficiency; if he is out of position he may be at only 95 per cent efficiency and that may be enough to give his opponent the edge.

There could come a time when you select a squad and choose your final XV on the day of the game, according to the conditions. It would only mean a change in the time element, with the team being announced rather nearer to the time of kick-off than is the custom; however I cannot see that method of selection being very popular with players in an amateur game. Players put in a tremendous amount of hard work to win a national place and they would be less than overwhelmed if they found there was no cap for them because it was raining. But the number of players likely to be affected by such a system would be very small and, given that the coach had been able to create a good squad atmosphere and that the

175

players knew what selection could involve, there is no reason why it should not work. Whether the advantages would offset the necessary adjustments to the teamwork established in the previous game is open to question.

There is no possibility of avoiding a generation gap between players and selectors. No matter how young your panel, their own playing days will be anywhere between five and fifteen years behind them so differences in attitude are bound to occur. But selectors should be able to get sufficiently close to players for a mutual relationship to evolve. The aims of the two, after all, are exactly the same. Players should feel that selectors are approachable, that opinions will be given a fair hearing; selectors, for their part, have the right to expect honesty in their chosen squad, to know that injuries will not be concealed. One might as well have an ideal objective, even if human frailties sometimes get in the way. It is when selectors change their regular habits at international weekends for no apparent reason, when they appear to be going out of their way to avoid players whom only the month before they were happy to laugh and joke with, that players begin to feel the ground shifting under them and confidence begins to wear thin. That was how it was for England in 1983.

In this respect I was pleased to hear that Derek Morgan was to succeed Budge Rogers as chairman of England's selectors in 1983. Derek was always ready to discuss matters with players and in conversations we had he and I did not always see eye to eye, but players knew they could expect a fair hearing from him and they would, in return, receive an honest expression of opinion. Sometimes you feel that selectors are frightened to commit themselves to a definite opinion for fear that it will not coincide with that of the chairman, or the Rugby Union committee, and might count as a black mark against them when the time comes for the following season's panel to be appointed.

Derek too, I am sure, will keep an eye on team discipline which, ultimately, is the chairman's responsibility, although he must rely on the team captain making his presence felt. It is the captain who must set the standard for the other players to follow, in commitment, in enthusiasm and in discipline, although it is not too much to hope for a collective responsibility among players who represent their country.

13

Cups and Coaching

For a club to reach the final of a national knockout competition in five years out of six argues a certain amount of consistency, not to say ability. Leicester were in the final of the John Player Cup in 1978, 1979, 1980, 1981 and 1983 and won the cup outright with three successive wins between 1979–81. Yet such achievements did not prevent critics of the club from saying that Leicester were lucky, or that they were the best of a poor bunch, or that they would never have made it without Dusty Hare's goal-kicking, all of which signalled a remarkable lack of generosity on their part for a quite singular reversal of fortunes.

Before 1978 Leicester had no cup record worth talking about. During the previous eight years we had enjoyed some good seasons but had done no more than reach the quarter-finals of the knockout competition in 1973. In 1976 we were forced to qualify for the following season's competition. Perhaps in those early days of the competition we made the mistake of thinking that cup rugby involved a change in style. Chalkie White, who had been involved in a lot of cup rugby in his own playing days, in Cumberland and Cornwall, counties where the local cup means a great deal, emphasized the fact that the side which makes the least mistakes wins through. Cup rugby was not to be played to the usual club pattern; our object was to tackle, to close the game down, and it was alien to our usual methods.

We learned, and I am sure that Chalkie learned, from that. If you grow used to playing in one way – and ours favoured open play – then it is difficult to switch styles for one odd game, whatever the prestige that may come from success. There is more at stake in a cup game, which can affect the more inhibited type of player, but by the late seventies we began to appreciate that cup rugby did not involve a change in emphasis. Not only that, we were all growing up. The youth-team players who had come into the side in 1975 had three years' experience under their belts, there were hardened 'senior professionals' like the wings, Bob Barker and John Duggan, internationals such as Robin Cowling, Dusty Hare and myself, and Paul Dodge had become an England player in 1978. By this time Chalkie had reached his most influential phase as a club coach and the material with which he had to work was growing richer.

Good luck came to our aid in 1978 too. For every match in the cup we were drawn at home. Our cup run that year attracted the attention of the curious and it did not take long for support to build up within the city and further afield. Our aims were modest. Our ambition was to reach the final but we never looked further than the next match until suddenly we had beaten Coventry (a sweet moment) in the semi-final and were packing our bags for Twickenham. By getting there we had achieved our ambition. It is frequently said that the worst round of a cup competition to lose is the semi-final because then you have nothing to show for your efforts, not even a loser's medal. Having reached the final we were obviously keen to win it but perhaps, subconsciously, we had done what we set out to do and we lost 6–3 to Gloucester.

Maybe it was necessary for us to reach and lose a final in order to understand properly what it takes to win the cup, though it was a sad day for some magnificent servants of the club – like Barker, Duggan and Bleddyn Jones – who did not have another opportunity to play in a final. It was suggested after the match that we 'froze' tactically and there is something in that. It was one of those games where we knew we were going to have problems of possession, that Gloucester's forward

179

strengths outweighed our own. We knew we had to use whatever ball we got in the best possible way and we did not. But then, when you get as little possession as we had in that final, it becomes difficult to sort out exactly what is the best way of using it. It was the biggest game of their careers for several of our players and some of them may not have been able to cope with it – other sides, I have no doubt, recognize the problems. Bristol could be said to have suffered from it in the first quarter of the 1983 final but they recovered much more quickly. All credit to them.

Despite defeat in 1978 we had all enjoyed the experience and the interest that it created in Leicester, so the following season we were that much more determined to win the cup. When we did so, by beating Moseley 15–12, it was one of the most memorable moments of an outstanding run of cup success. We came from behind in a cliff-hanging game to make up substantially for the disappointment of the previous year. The joy of that moment was parallelled by our third successive win, that over Gosforth in 1981. We had beaten London Irish in the 1980 final 21–9 but it was by no means an exciting game, whereas against Gosforth very few gave us much prospect of success. We would struggle up front, we were told; we responded to the challenge, Gosforth were not at their best and we won 22–15 in a game of movement and life which reflected, we felt, the style of rugby we tried to play all the time. It meant so much more to us because it occurred at the end of our centenary season and we were allowed to keep the cup permanently. It meant a vast amount, too, to the club's officials and supporters, for whom the cup had now established a tradition of support.

The membership had built up rapidly over the first two years of cup success but it was not only the cup that was responsible. We had acquired more good players since our first final, Les Cusworth and Clive Woodward, and people in Leicester and Leicestershire began to appreciate that they would see good rugby week after week at Welford Road. They may have come initially because of the cup but they stayed and soon the membership began to be numbered in thousands rather than hundreds. We began to hear of groups of supporters who would book coaches for the final as early as January, which showed a sublime optimism. If talk in the clubhouse ever turned to the formation of leagues someone was bound to say: 'What do you need leagues for, we've got the cup?' without appreciating that if you get knocked out of the cup in the first round, the competition itself does not fulfil English rugby's need for a more competitive structure.

The fact that the Leicester club had made changes to its internal structure in the mid-seventies helped us cope with the flood of interest which might have made another club wilt under such a huge burden. We have always been lucky to have the Barbarians fixture which was an ideal proving ground for the cup. Administrators were accustomed to dealing with big crowds at least once every year and that provided a formula whereby we could keep pace with our development as a cup side. The players were able to identify how much work was going on behind the scenes by the efforts that were made to ensure trouble-free preparation for the games and to ensure that the players themselves felt they were the ones who mattered and responded accordingly.

But even in the midst of so much hard work and so much success which, on some occasions, we felt many supporters were coming to take for granted, we never gave our cup opponents anything less than total respect. We never expected automatically to reach the final which indicates how well the players had matured as a team. We were always aware of our own weaknesses and how we could be beaten. Fortunately very few sides uncovered those weak areas in cup games – some perhaps did not even look for them. We may sometimes have given our opponents too much respect but we knew, once we had won the cup, how keen every other club in the country would be to beat us. When we did eventually

181

lose, after winning eighteen successive cup games, it was to Moseley in the 1982 semi-finals when we played untidily and went down to two penalties and two dropped goals against a try scored by Cusworth.

During that run of eighteen games there was one occasion when an air of gloom descended on Welford Road and I had the definite feeling that, this time, we were on our way out. We had been drawn at home to Bristol in the second round of the 1981 competition and after appearing in three finals, winning two of them, many of us felt that this might be our come-uppance. Bristol were and are a good side. They have been worthy opposition ever since I have been involved in first-class rugby and that week the weather was foul. The rain was lashing down as I drove down to the ground and conditions seemed to favour their bigger forwards rather than our backs. When I had parked the car I saw Jerry Day, the secretary, and asked him to put the cup itself into the changing room. I thought it would focus the attention of our players on what was at stake because the cup had come to mean so much to all of us and, at the end of the day, it was something tangible for the side that came out in front.

We went out for the game and in the first few minutes David Sorrell, the Bristol fly half, missed a kick at goal from right in front. Whether the sense of occasion affected his nerves I cannot say but, where their place-kickers had a poor day, Dusty kicked everything and we won 27–14. We had a hard quarter-final that year too, against Sale, but perhaps the knowledge that it was our centenary season helped to bring a little extra from the players. We were so lucky that our third cup win coincided with our hundredth birthday – being able to keep the cup was a marvellous culmination to the season. In some ways it was irrelevant that the centenary should have occurred then because the club was developing its rugby the way we wanted, but if we had written the script ourselves for 1980–81 we could not have asked for a better denouement.

There were worries before the season began about our ability to last the course. We began training early in June 1980 because of the tour to Australia and Fiji which began in August. It was an incredibly long season and it was felt that, by April 1981, we might be just a little jaded. But as the season neared its end we were buoyed up by a succession of newspaper awards and trophies. We came through a very testing semi-final with London Scottish (which went to extra time) and we knew that Gosforth, our opponents at Twickenham, had pushed Moseley all over the place in winning their semi-final 24–3. Already the papers were talking about how our forwards would suffer in comparison with Gosforth. Hard luck, Leicester, seemed to be the line. You've done well but this time it's Gosforth for the cup.

At the training session which followed the London Scottish game all the players agreed that we would take the final three weeks of the season as methodically as possible. The alternatives which faced us were to make the season into the most memorable one in the club's history or to see all our hard work fizzle away. We buckled down to training as hard as we had ever done, we did well against Welsh opposition over Easter and – remarkably, since we were cup holders – went in against Gosforth as underdogs. My job as captain was made so much easier by the predictions of the pundits and we won 22–15, playing the rugby that people expected us to play. It was the last game for two fine players, Cowling and Adey (who had been persuaded to postpone retirement) and everyone played their part. Dusty scored fourteen points and two of our non-international backs, Steve Kenney and Tim Barnwell, scored superb tries. Memories of the qualities that such players as those two have brought to the club are made more poignant by that grotesquely unlucky accident suffered by Tim in the 1983 final against Bristol, which put him into hospital needing an operation to clear a blood clot on the brain and effectively ended his first-class playing career.

I think during that centenary season we could justifiably have claimed to be the best club side in England. We were a match for anyone at Welford Road and there were only two or three clubs we would have worries about visiting. I do not think we could have made that claim at any other time between 1978 and 1983. During the other years that we won the cup people could say: 'Yes, Leicester won the cup but so-and-so were the best club in the country.' Without a league system you have no way of assessing in cast-iron fashion which is truly the best club in the country because it has to be acknowledged that, in a cup competition, clubs may get a bad draw, not perform well and depart the cup scene at an early stage. The classic example of that is Bristol in 1982. They lost to Liverpool at home in the second round of the cup, a game they really should have won, and then beat everyone else, ourselves included, out of sight. But during our three cup wins, the 'so-and-so' who others claimed were the best in the country would have changed each year. I do not believe any other club had the capacity to do so consistently what we did. That happened through a combination of circumstances: the organizational ability was there off the field, the playing talent was available on the field. We were able to play the kind of rugby people will come and watch because we happened to have three international midfield players and an international fullback who loved to run the ball. We had a running scrum half too. If we had possessed five international tight forwards it might have been different but as it was we simply had an adequate pack.

Nothing suits forwards better than to find themselves written off, as has happened to us time and again. You would have thought the critics would have learned after a while, considering that for much of our cup run the Leicester forwards included three full internationals, two B internationals and a clutch of under-23 players. Week in and week out Leicester's was not a dominating pack, except against mediocre opposition. Though our jumpers can usually manage an outstanding effort on the big occasions we seldom take charge at the line-out, but people should watch our scrummaging more closely. Although we have not had a big pack we have always scrummaged low and well, making up in technique what we lacked in sheer bulk. Scrummaging is largely a matter of hard work and one of our main theories has always been that we must be able to rely on getting set-piece ball from at least one area and that is the scrum.

This does not mean we concede the line-out but we accepted that, against sides like Gosforth in 1981 and Bristol in 1983, we were unlikely to get much more than 35 per cent possession in that area – it would have been silly to try to pretend otherwise. So we must get clean ball from the scrummage or we fall down. A lot of our set moves behind the scrum are based on that theory and also on the knowledge that we should win a fair share of second-phase possession, either through mauling it off the opposition or by having three-quarters who are strong and skilful enough to stand up that much longer in the tackle and wait for the back row to arrive and carry on movements.

The personnel may have changed over the last six years but the success rate has been maintained. Would it have happened if we had not been coached by Chalkie White? No one can say, though I suspect we would not have achieved the degree of consistency that we did. He had no serious rival for the post during his stay at Leicester and though many people deserve a share of the credit for what the club has done, the lion's share must go to him. His influence was vast, not only on the team but on players as individuals. His dedication to the game is exceptional. He loves the game as an art form, for the potential that any eighty minutes may bring, not merely as an exercise to be reduced by a coach to the nuts and bolts. The mental and physical preparation he puts into games has been phenomenal. He worked on the game at home, he took training, he attended committee meetings, he went to matches; in an amateur game he gave of himself far more than anyone had the right to expect, certainly more than the players – and *their* contribution is far from negligible these days. He sees himself as a visionary which accounts for his gift of being able to plan the game long-term. While we were training for the start of the season he would have sketched out how the season would end but, more than that, the clarity of his foresight allowed him to identify the pitfalls and the rewards which the game would throw up during the next five to ten years. That is an ability afforded to very few.

As a player, at Borough Road College, at Camborne and with Leicester, he was a scrum half, and when he became a coach he was happy to leave much of the work of the pack in training to the senior forwards. When he began players like David Matthews, Bob Rowell, Roger Grove (now coach to Moseley) and Graham Willars – his eventual successor – were there. When they retired Robin Cowling and I took over, then Steve Johnson, and now Ian Smith, captain for the 1983–84 season, will help out Graham. As back-row forwards both, they should form a sympathetic team.

Chalkie would make points to the forwards that he felt necessary, generally relating to the game we had just played or the game we were about to play, then he would leave the scrum and line-out to the forwards. When it came to rucking and mauling he was more creative and insistent. When I began at Leicester the development of second-phase skills left much to be desired. We would practise arrowheads – running mauls – for hours, until we were heartily sick of them, until one day we found that we were doing things instinctively. No longer was it a mechanical process, first man goes in this side of the ball-carrier, second man that side and so on. We found as we were running up to loose situations that we had assessed the situation before arrival and had come to the appropriate conclusion about where we could best lend our efforts.

During the course of any one match, very few rucks and mauls are exactly the same. Players have to look for the points of check and balance and make their own decisions over where to join in. Only by going through all

186

the different options week after week – and it takes years to assimilate all of them – do you reach the position where players react in the most advantageous way to what they see happening in front of them. You must not tell this prop, or that lock, that his job is always to do such-and-such. You must reach the position where every forward knows the best thing to do. It frightens me to think of the number of man-hours Chalkie made us put into achieving this. Eventually the players adapted to the demands made by the coach. Everything became a degree easier and at last we knew that we were approaching the state of fitness and mental agility which Chalkie was seeking.

One of his skills was the identification of players' virtues and vices – in a playing sense. He would use their virtues to best advantage within the context of the team but he would never ask a player to perform a skill which was beyond him. He would be quite frank about this with players. He would tell them not to attempt certain moves because they would either not perform them well enough or, in some cases, would not be capable of performing them at all. Sometimes the instruction would emerge as a joke but the players always got the message.

One of his sayings has almost passed into rugby legend: 'Let others tell you how good you are, I'll tell you how to be better.' He would praise individuals for some aspect of their game but you would always be aware that other aspects needed working on. One of our games that he really cherished was the cup semi-final against Wasps in 1979 which we won 43–7, but he said very little afterwards except to indicate that all the training, all the hard work, had for once paid off in an outstanding display of fluid rugby. I think we knew he was pleased.

We knew, too, when he was less than pleased. In his early days as coach his man-management was one of his weaknesses. After a bad game he would storm into the changing room, tense from the emotion of the game, pointing the finger at the dropped pass, the bad kick. Once he literally rapped a player's knuckles: he was

187

running the line and had to watch as Bob Barker dropped a try-scoring pass and when the whistle for half-time blew a few seconds later he came on the field with the oranges and cracked the touch flag over Bob's hand. Players know best of all when they have played badly; very few of them need it pointing out to them immediately the game has ended. Yet the job of a coach must be terrible for he lacks the release of tension provided by actually playing the game. Chalkie became intensely wound up in games and he had to sit on the sidelines, watching the players bringing to nought all the hard work they and he had put into preparing for the game.

But he learned, too, from his own mistakes. He remained very vocal during the course of games and his stentorian tones would ring out if he saw any player doing something worthy of congratulation. He learned to take himself away from the players after a bad performance, perhaps to share a cup of tea with the groundsman and listen to the football results on the radio for twenty minutes while the players stripped off their kit and dispersed to the bath. By that time the element of confrontation had been dispelled. Chalkie became more philosophical. He never suffered fools gladly but he learned to put up with them for the good qualities they might have to offer to the game. He never, for one moment, stopped treating players as individuals.

We could have lost Chalkie halfway through our cup run, if England had asked him to coach the national side in 1979. That would have shown how much we were worth without him, since at that time we had lost one and won one in terms of cup finals. We knew he was in the running for the job but, despite our awareness of his ability, it was never felt at Leicester that he was a certainty to get it. We all had a smattering of knowledge about the workings of the Rugby Union and Chalkie has never been the greatest diplomat in the world, especially when it comes to the preparation of teams for representative matches. He always knows exactly what he wants for his players, and which players he needs for the task in hand, and he does not mind treading on people's toes to get them. Nor was he ever slow to tell people if he thought they were wrong and why he thought they were wrong.

But the job would have been absolutely right for him at that stage. He had all the credentials, he had the track record, he had worked successfully with players at club and representative level and won their respect – not just the respect of players from the Midlands but of those from all over the country. As an ambitious individual the timing was right too. There was little more he could achieve at club level and the natural progression was to coach England. I know he wanted to do the job very much. We also knew that, if he did get the job, the hardest part of it would be to give up his connection with Leicester.

Had he been given the chance it would have put him in line to coach the 1983 Lions in New Zealand though, in my own mind, I am sure that the 1980 tour to South Africa was made for him. The hard grounds are ideal for running rugby and whenever I have heard him talk about back play, however senior the company, I have become utterly convinced that he can get more out of a set of backs than any other coach I know. He would have fitted in so well with Syd Millar as manager and Billy Beaumont as captain, both of them forwards. As it is, on both the 1980 and the 1983 tours he arrived in time to watch the last two tests in a losing series as no more than an observer. It was a cruel waste of talent at a time when the touring backs desperately needed a touch of inspiration.

The Rugby Union decided, in their wisdom, that Mike Davis should coach England, a man with a proven record in coaching schoolboys but as yet little achievement at senior level. It would have been no bad thing if Mike had been made assistant to Chalkie. He could have benefited so much from the experience, could perhaps have taken charge of the under-23s, and would have been in total command of the situation when the time came for

189

Chalkie to step down. When Chalkie was rejected we took it as a snub for Leicester from rugby's establishment, perhaps because Chalkie's views did not coincide with those in authority, perhaps because we at Leicester had a reputation for being anti-county championship.

It is richly ironic that Chalkie's next step was to become an employee of the Rugby Union, when he became technical administrator for the South and South-West in 1983. Now he and his colleagues, Alan Old, David Shaw (both of whom played for Leicester) and Barrie Corless have a greatly widened sphere of influence. They can bring home a telling message to the captains and coaches in their areas; very few, I am sure, could fail to be influenced by Chalkie. He has done thousands of sessions at Leicester, he has come up with the answers to questions which many people have only just begun to realize exist. It is impossible to resist the observation that he had only been at his base in Taunton for four months when the South and South-West (in the shape of the Bristol club) added the John Player Cup to the county championship that the same area (Gloucestershire) had already won at the start of the year!

As a twenty-year-old, living away from home for the first time in my life, it will surprise no one to learn that I was much influenced by Chalkie. Initially the relationship tended to be that of master and pupil but it broadened, after I became club captain, into something more akin to father and son. We held long and frequent conversations about rugby, about life, about attitudes. He knocked away my immaturity and set standards for me, as he did for everyone. I always believed that coaches had to have some special quality and while there may be coaches as good as he – no one is indispensable – I doubt if many of them will encompass all his human qualities. If there are I will not be in a position to know them as well as I know Chalkie, or to offer them a similar acknowledgement.

14

League of Gentlemen?

I have said that Leicester's attitude towards the county championship may have counted against Chalkie as far as coaching England was concerned. It is only fair to say that Chalkie never led the players in that direction. It was an attitude which grew up during the mid-seventies after general dissatisfaction with the standard of rugby played in the championship in our area. We began to appreciate that the club could offer everything the players wanted in rugby-playing terms and that the county championship only hindered club performances. In the Midlands at that time county games were played on Wednesday evenings; they disrupted regular Monday and Thursday training sessions at Leicester and took players straight from a hard day's work to some pretty mixed venues. Not only were the performances of individual players sub-standard, they affected performances for the club on the following Saturday.

I had been brought up to regard county rugby as a respectable objective which, when I was playing rugby in London with a junior club, it was. That feeling did not change when I moved to the Midlands, and I discovered that the county still provided a decent objective for junior clubs. During my last season of county rugby in 1974 I captained the Leicestershire side and found it composed of a large number of enthusiastic, committed players from clubs such as Loughborough Town, Kibworth and Westleigh plus a sprinkling of senior players. We did fairly well that season in the Midland group, we organized extra training sessions to see if we could reach

191

the knockout stage and then we went to Burton to play Staffordshire. It was a match we could have won but we lost it after what, in my view, was a series of amazing decisions from the referee. He, at least, appeared to be enjoying himself and said as much to me at half-time. I sat down in the changing room after the game was over, seething with frustration. The championship was supposed to be the bridge between club and country and yet they could not even give us a decent official. I decided then that, if that was county rugby, the Rugby Union could keep it.

There are twenty-seven county championship sides and if you said there were two dozen genuine first-class clubs in the country you might be stretching a point, whatever the official designations of the Rugby Union suggest. So there must be some intermingling of senior and junior players in the championship which is not going to raise standards for the players from whom the representative sides will come. I agree with the view that there should be some intermediary stage between club and country and the divisional tournament, which was introduced in the second half of the seventies, provided it. When it began the North quickly established some sense of identity, largely because they were based on the successful Lancashire side and because they instituted short tours to prepare for the engagements to come. The Midlands could have developed a similar spirit.

But the competition ran for one season, in 1977–78, was held over for the following two seasons because of the presence of touring sides, played in 1980–81 and was then abandoned because, it was said, the public had little opportunity to identify with it. I dare say this was true since the tournament took place so infrequently. It is just such a competition that would give better preparation for those sides who play touring teams. After all, with major tours being shortened to eighteen matches it will always be divisional sides in England that will play, so why not give them a better prospect of doing well? At the same time a divisional tournament serves the purpose of taking promising players out of their club setting and seeing how they flourish in better company. All too frequently the county championship serves only to take club players and put them with lesser company.

This is not to deny the county championship a function. It has one, and an important one. It should be open to players from junior clubs and those senior club players not involved in the first-team squad. It could be played regionally, as it used to be, to keep down expenses and it would represent a definite step up for the players involved. As things stand, if the Leicester first-teamers make themselves available they provide virtually the whole of the county side, just as they did when Leicestershire won the county championship in the 1920s. What incentive is there then for junior-club players if they know that all county places will be filled from the senior club? Then you find counties having to create another team, at additional expense, to cater for the needs of the junior players. In Leicestershire there is a county Barbarians team which fulfils that need.

It has been claimed that, if you remove the seniority of their competition, then you detract from the position of county officials. I cannot think why. They are involved in rugby to help with the administration of all clubs within their particular orbit and if that administration involved county games at a lower playing level than currently, they would still be performing yeoman service. Any player that shone in the championship could be encouraged to join a senior club which, again, may cause a degree of heartache among junior-club officials but would be the best course for the player concerned.

Any official involved in English rugby has two basic questions to ask themselves: do they want to play in the old traditions of the game, to look after their own parish and never see beyond it, or do they want to help produce the best possible national side? To me the two are not compatible. If you want to play county championship rugby as it stands and keep your fixtures as they have always been, do not start complaining when England

193

lose three or four matches a season. The leading players are not being given the chance to play as well as they possibly can often enough because the playing structure of the game is wrong.

Surely that is indicated by the number of times the Rugby Union has to review the county championship and try to breath new life into it, as they did last season. Leicester and the other leading Midland clubs all received a letter from the Rugby Union president, J.V. Smith, saying that they should make their grounds and players available for the county championship. It was so heavy-handed that it annoyed people who had previously been fairly neutral on the club v. county issue. Players are not obliged to play for a team if they do not want to. Furthermore there was no justification, either on local or national grounds, for a restructured county competition in which we did not believe. In the view of most Midland clubs it simply interfered with several of our better club fixtures on Saturdays. Would the selectors learn more from watching Leicestershire against Hertfordshire, which was one fixture clash in 1982?

The only way to ensure that standards rise is to bring the best elements in the national game together in a league system. The best players, the best coaches, the best administrators would gravitate towards the most successful clubs where the players could be sure of playing their best rugby as often as possible. The business of fitting leagues into the season is merely an administrative detail. If you have willing people who accept the basic principle and want to make it happen, then it will happen.

Broadly speaking you could have two top divisions, with regional feeder divisions, playing ten games in the first half of the season, i.e. during October, November and December. That would lead directly into divisional or trial games and the international championship which could be interspersed, as it is now, by the cup competition. Obviously you must establish the criteria for the top twenty-two clubs in the country which would form your top two divisions and, having done so, officials from clubs who were not chosen would be up in arms in protest. But since you have promotion and relegation within your league, any mistakes in the selection of the top twenty-two would be ironed out within three years as clubs found their natural level.

Any side that complains about lack of recognition has an obvious answer: work harder and justify a place at someone else's expense. Some clubs have already realized what is required in the modern game after years of sitting on their assets. Blackheath and Harlequins are two such clubs; fifty years ago their fixtures and their position within the game were the envy of the country but they sat back and allowed their premier position to be eroded. Both have worked very hard over the last few years to remedy that and their results of the last two seasons indicate how well they have succeeded. At the other end of the scale you have a club such as Orrell who worked desperately hard for years to break into the first-class circuit. Helped in part by the cup, they have now just about achieved their wish.

It would be possible to go on and on suggesting schemes for a league system but there is no need. The Rugby Union have a series of blueprints gathering dust at Twickenham and it is unfortunate that the major clubs have tripped themselves up in their own 'old boy' network. While the Rugby Union have constantly worked to preserve the county championship, the major clubs have, by and large, agreed to maintain the meaningless merit tables in the knowledge that, if they opt for a proper league system, some of their number will fall by the way because they have not established nor the organization to cope with inclusion. One of the most popular arguments is the financial one: if, say, Leicester have a bad season in the league and are relegated it would drastically reduce their income, but that argument is one of shameful timidity. If Leicester, or any other club, has a bad season, the level of support drops anyway as does the amount of money coming into the

195

club. Sponsorship depends on success and the more work you put into making the club a success, the more support you will attract. The clubs that work hardest, whether on or off the field, deserve the rewards, whether they are Orrell, Hinkley or whoever.

No club should have the right to reach a premier position in the country and then sit back and enjoy the view. If that happens you will start to go backwards in any case. Players will not be attracted to an unambitious, unimaginative club because it will not create the right atmosphere for them to realize their potential. It is conceivable that some clubs might agree to merge in order to produce a more viable and successful unit but, strictly speaking, I do not think it is necessary. If clubs wanted to enter the league scene, they would organize themselves sufficiently well to do so; how they did it would be up to them and would be influenced by their own geography.

Young players or junior-club players whose careers blossom comparatively late must be given the opportunity to get into a first-class club where they can learn the game among the better players and from the better coaches, from July to the following April. Players of potential can derive nothing from a county set-up where they have a few training sessions and a handful of games over a six-week period. At Leicester members of the youth team or the Swifts train alongside internationals every week, from whom they can learn so much. During the first half of the season there would be the sense of purpose induced by the efforts to win promotion to the second division, to the first division, or to win the division championship. All the games would be highly competitive, few if any would be lost to the weather and the players would be required to play their best rugby directly before the international season. Standards would improve, particularly for those clubs who may now play mediocre fixtures. Players from such clubs are being asked to make an unreasonable leap in standards when faced by a side of international class.

196

If anyone is worried about the travel problems of clubs such as Gosforth and Camborne, I doubt if there would be much difficulty in finding a company to sponsor the league so that costs would present no headache. If Thorn EMI are prepared to pay a considerable sum of money into a county championship which does not begin to function, then commerce would be fighting to sponsor a well-structured league system. Indeed, a sponsor was found last season for a super-league which was planned but never came into operation. I am sure that a league would impose no more burdens on clubs and players than they should be prepared to face anyway. It would certainly make life more difficult for us at Leicester because clubs would be so much better organized than they are now and, consequently, harder to beat!

Nationally, however, the effects would be marked. You might find, particularly in the north, that one club had attracted better players because it was the only one in the first division. Ambitious players recognizing an ambitious club would go there in the hope of enhancing their prospects of playing for England. That again is only an extension of what is beginning to happen now. Players like Les Cusworth, Clive Woodward and Nick Youngs wanted to get on in their rugby so they joined Leicester and either put up with travelling from outside the county – as Les does – or found themselves jobs nearby.

Perhaps too many people in this country have been brought up to regard competition as taboo, to think of leagues as a dirty word. I do not pretend to know when is the best time to introduce competition to players; in New Zealand seven and eight-year-olds have their own competitive structure which may impose too great a strain on them (or on their parents). But it took England a hundred years to introduce one major cup – and even then they called it a knockout competition. It had teething problems but now, after eleven years, it is beginning to catch on.

What effect would the injection of more money have on the clubs? It is, I suppose, possible that some unscrupulous official might offer players inducements to join his club in the hope of improving their league position, but the way that rugby clubs work I doubt if that would happen. Rule by committee may not always be the best way of ordering things but it does impose a system of checks on any individual who may wish to steamroller his way over others. Clubs have always wanted to attract the best players and have found ways of doing so without offering straight cash inducements. Usually this has taken the form of finding job opportunities for players who are known to want to move into the area.

The rest of England's representative apparatus seems somewhat involved. I have never taken too much notice of the doings of England's B and under-23 teams, possibly because I never played for either of them myself. But those are not the only stepping stones to a full cap. England have taken to playing what they term an England XV against countries who are deemed not to merit a full international; this is a further opportunity to experiment, while the England Students, being of much the same age, duplicate the sort of fixtures which the under-23s might aim at. Maybe you do need a link between England's eighteen-group school side and the senior internationals but I believe a divisional tournament would go a long way towards providing that link. If it was felt a B team was justified, then would it not be better for them to play more than one fixture a season? There is no reason why a B team should not play regular fixtures against the continental countries. England did so against Romania in 1978, Wales took what they called a B squad to Spain in 1983. This is just the kind of recognition that many of the European Rugby Federation (FIRA) countries seek.

A final thought on the structure of our game. While John Burgess was travelling up and down the country preparing a report for the Rugby Union on how the quality of English rugby might be improved he visited the England squad while they were training at Bisham

Abbey. He asked the players' opinions and I was surprised to find players from the north speaking out in favour of a club league. All of them admitted that they loved county rugby, that they might not have reached such heights in the game but for exposure through county rugby, but they recognized that what seemed good for them was not necessarily right for the rest of the country. John and his fellow committee members went round the country several times trying to discover what clubs, senior and junior, felt about the game, and his reports were discussed by the Rugby Union and then fed back again to the constituent bodies and clubs for comment. In the end the clubs grew bored with it all and the consequence was that they were said to be apathetic on the question of leagues. It was a classic example of the old saying: if you ask the same question often enough, in the end you will get the answer you want.

15

All in the Game

It would be idle to pretend that everything is blooming in rugby's garden. Most of those involved in the game, from high to low, are aware that it is not. The problems that face the game's authorities are greater than ever before and they all stem from rugby's growing popularity, which has brought in its train vastly increased exposure from the press, radio and television. The concomitant of enhanced media exposure is an upsurge in the marketing power possessed by the game which the authorities are a long way from harnessing. This, in turn, leads on to the possibility which has exercised so many minds in 1983 – professional rugby union.

'Perks' have been available to players for many years and though the authorities tend to look at the rules regarding amateurism as writ large in black and white, I believe the definition of the amateur player has become increasingly blurred, not over the last two or three years but over the last decade. One aspect of the whole furore surrounding amateur status remains perfectly clear: the players want no financial reward for playing rugby. If they have become at all 'professional', it is in their preparation for the game as compared with those who played twenty, thirty, or forty years ago.

This may be part and parcel of the social changes which have taken place in England since the Second World War. I have no qualifications as a sociologist but it would be true to say that, in the eighties, many men find themselves offered greater responsibilities in their careers at a younger age than in the sixties. The pressure imposed by the game itself may not have increased dramatically over the last twenty years but it obviously requires more time, and those who play it – and at the top level that is basically men aged between twenty and thirty – do so while coping with additional strains in their careers. A generation ago it is reasonable to suppose that a man's playing days would be all but over before he saw his career develop when he was in his mid-thirties.

As a generalization, three main elements occupy the time of the average rugby-playing Briton: his family, his career and his rugby. If one of those elements comes to assume a greater degree of importance, it necessarily deprives the remaining two elements. International rugby is demanding; it is therefore the responsibility of the game's authorities to cushion the blow which falls upon players' families and employers who are, at the moment, subsidizing rugby up and down the country, the one in terms of time and help given to wives and children, the other in terms of time and money. Wives are naturally proud of their husband's achievements but it becomes no easier for players to cross evening after evening off the domestic diary.

That is the background to the 'scandals' which have come to light over the last few years: direct cash inducement by rival sports equipment firms to persuade players to wear their brand of boots, inflated expenses paid to internationals turning out for an exhibition game or speaking at a dinner. The sums of money in all these cases are very small and no player is likely to require a numbered account in Zurich or a tax haven in the West Indies to cope with them. Nevertheless the money becomes available to players because of their rugby, and clearly transgresses existing rules of the game.

But, as I have said, there have always been inducements available to players; the difference now is that the inducement is a clearly identifiable cash present, in the case of boot money because that is the easiest and most practical way of stealing a march on your business rival.

201

Rumours of money circulating within the game in Wales and France have abounded as long as I can remember but today no one country in the five nations championship can put their hand on their heart and claim that their game is blameless.

Players do not become aware of the 'perks' available until they approach international standard. I certainly did not. It came as a surprise when someone handed me a new pair of boots because I was a member of England's squad and, as a newcomer, you do not stop to question his action. You are grateful only for the equipment and though even the newest of new boys realizes that the motives behind the gift are not entirely philanthropic, you question no further. This has now become standard practice. Firms will offer equipment, boots, track suits, jerseys and holdalls to clubs and to national squads because it is worth their while. The gifts are accepted, just as they are when offered after international matches, just as they are when Rugby Union committeemen are invited with their wives on what amounts to the cheapest of holidays with substantial momentoes thrown in at the end of their visit to South Africa or wherever.

Where do you begin to make your distinction? Where is the amateur line breached? Is it in the plush hotels, the good food and high living on tour, the entertainments, the gifts, or must it always be pinned to grubby pound notes? At the moment, however, this is only a question of semantics. The facts are that players discovered taking money will be banned for life. I do not know who the first person was to accept boot money – whoever it was must have thought long and hard before he came to his decision – but it only needed one to start the trend and others will have followed suit. Those who did so will have come to their own arrangements with the manufacturer's representative and, for obvious reasons, will not have talked to all and sundry about it.

I gather that in some Rugby Union circles I am regarded as the 'shop steward' for the players, which might suggest some connivance on my part as regards the arrangements for the payment of boot money. But that title, such as it was, was conferred largely through the coincidence that it was a friend of mine who became the Adidas representative for rugby equipment in this country. Robin Money and I had shared a flat during my early days at Leicester, but after his playing days as a fullback with Leicester were over Robin changed jobs and moved to Wilmslow to work for Adidas.

A year or two later it became obvious to the England squad that players from the north were arriving at sessions with new equipment which they collected from the Adidas factory at Pointon. The company were happy to offer players and selectors free kit and no one was going to turn the offer down. Naturally enough players from elsewhere in the country were curious to know whether there was the odd track suit or sweater available for them and, since I was a friend of Robin's, they asked me what the chances were of a general distribution of kit. It then became merely a question of coordination so as to make an equitable arrangement for all concerned. I took the 'orders', as it were, passed them on to Robin, and he would generally leave the equipment with me for distribution to the squad members. Adidas were happy for England players to be seen wearing their clothing on international occasions and the players were more than happy to wear it, without ever feeling they were a walking billboard for the company. Everyone in authority knew of the practice and accepted it.

That was the extent of my 'stewardship'. I never became a spokesman for the players in any other way because that was not my function. That was the captain's role, or the chairman of selectors' role, and had nothing to do with me. Of course I expressed my views on matters relating to the squad as any senior team member would do and those views would sometimes have to do with the arrangements made for players. I have always said that the players must be relieved of as many cares as possible so that they can deliver their best rugby on the day and there were lots of restrictions which

I considered petty and in which I tried to bring about improvements.

A few examples will do. The Rugby Union should ensure that players' wives are looked after on international match days and in my opinion that extends to paying the bill for their hotel on the Saturday nights. To be fair, much has been done in that direction over the last two years, but I can remember Margaret coming upon the wives of the Welsh players standing in the rain after one international at Twickenham because no one had made arrangements to look after them until the players were free. She managed to get them into one of the restaurants, but it would not be asking too much for one official to be designated to ensure the wives' comfort before, during and after games. They, too, could be made to feel special on international occasions because much of the supporting role falls on their shoulders when players are away. The players would then leave home on the Thursday before the game happy in the knowledge that when their wives arrived at the appointed spot in London, there would be a Rugby Union representative present to welcome them and ensure that they were provided for and equipped with a ticket for the match. That would leave each player free to concentrate on the game, rather than wondering whether members of his family were running round London looking for transport and means of entrance to Twickenham.

Telephone calls, too, within reason, should fall within the Union's province. The sort of thing I have in mind is the occasion when I received from the Rugby Union a letter asking for payment of a telephone bill of just over £9 contracted while I was with the squad in Edinburgh before a game with Scotland. Players are expected to give up two working days and two family days for internationals so it seems reasonable that, during those four days, you should be able to make at least one call to your employer and one to your home – which is what I had done on that occasion. I simply was not prepared to pay for those calls and if the Rugby Union wanted to take me

204

to court over them, as at one time seemed a possibility, I would have been happy to attend. The bill should have been part of the overall hotel bill and, as such, paid by the Rugby Union.

Another of my pet niggles was practice balls. Nearly all first-class clubs these days play with an all-weather Mitre ball but, for international matches at Twickenham, they revert to the leather Gilbert balls. The two makes have different characteristics, in flight, in handling and kicking, and it seemed essential for players, during training on the Thursday and Friday before an international, and at Stourbridge during Monday squad sessions, to train in conditions as near as possible to those of the international. We needed new Gilbert balls, one for the forwards and one for the backs – not old Gilberts, nor even nearly new Gilberts, because once a leather ball has been used at all its weight and its shape change drastically, particularly if it has been used in wet conditions.

I kept on bothering Don Rutherford, the Rugby Union's technical administrator, about this until one day he appeared at a session with a new Gilbert. Both of us were delighted, Don because he hoped I would stop nagging him, me because at last it seemed I had helped a little towards preparing the squad better. I turned the ball over and found a little stamp on it: 'Reject – Imperfect'. You can't win. I even spoke to Rod Webb, the former England wing who now works with Gilbert at their factory in Rugby, about supplying new practice balls; I was assured that we could have as many as we wanted but still, so far as I am aware, the matter remains unresolved.

Now all these things are little things and may not seem, in isolation, to count for much. But life is made up of little, comparatively unimportant things which, taken together, can make a considerable impact. I have to confess, also, that I once made off from Twickenham with a match ball that the Rugby Union were kind enough to let me keep. It was the ball with which the

John Player Cup final was played one year. I had promised to bring it back to Leicester so that it could be raffled in order to raise money for a school for mentally handicapped children in the city. When the final whistle blew I stuck the ball up my jersey and, back in the changing room, transferred it to my kitbag. Almost immediately a groundsman entered, asking for the return of the ball. I explained why I wanted it but he said he had to have the ball before his duty was completed for the day. Off he went and returned shortly with the ball, my explanation having been accepted by the secretary. The Rugby Union are human too!

All of which may seem to be taking us a long way from the central issue of boot money and other payments made to players, which can most charitably be described as inflated expenses. However hard I try, I cannot regard them as illegitimate and threatening to the game. The players involved are a very small percentage of the playing population and the extra responsibilities which they shoulder because of their achievements within the game are deserving of some compensation. Let us take the invitation to speak at a club dinner, which almost all players find demanding, myself among them. The invited player may accept the date, six months away, only to find that when it comes to the week concerned, he has two nights' training with his own club, a match to play, an extra squad session thrown in – plus the dinner. It leaves very little time for the family that week and may mean his employer making do in his absence, or colleagues covering for him because he has to leave his job early to travel to the dinner.

Yet it is not a burden on the player himself. He may be unenthusiastic about preparing a speech to give to people whom he has never met before, but once there the company is familiar enough because rugbymen everywhere have so many points in common. Whatever expenses the speaker may be paid are generally used (if he has any diplomacy at all) in softening the blow of his continual absence from home. Presumably the presence of a leading player enhances the occasion for the club who invited him and by no means all players would go to dinners expecting some financial return. In the same way players accepting invitations to appear in exhibition games, to celebrate the opening of a clubhouse or a golden jubilee, are able to give junior clubs a day they will long remember. The junior players will prize the day they played against a team of internationals, who in turn may serve to boost rugby in that particular locality. Everyone benefits in the playing sense – but it does mean another Sunday away from the family.

No, the burden is shouldered by the family and by employers. I am convinced that firms who allow their employees ten or twelve weeks off to go on a major tour, or four weeks on a short tour, should receive compensation for the loss of their staff. There are very few tours of major countries which fail to make a profit, in most cases an extremely healthy profit. Players' salaries should be offered to the employers out of the tour profits, which might have the dual effect of ensuring that countries were able to take their strongest playing party abroad. How many times have sides left Britain regretting the absence of players unable to tour because their jobs make it impossible? And how many players, like Clive Williams and Dougie Morgan, have given up pay, in some instances jobs, in order to be able to accept the invitation to become a Lion? And anyone who sniffs and says that, at a time when there are three million unemployed people, they should get their priorities right, fails to appreciate the single-mindedness and dedication needed to reach international status. Rugby players require just as much dedication as any top professional sportsmen, but, unlike the professionals, do not see the huge financial rewards coming their way. They do not want those rewards; for me, 50 per cent of the pleasure of the game has always been the social side. But players, though they are prepared to make sacrifices, do not want to constantly ask others to do the same, just so that they can give of their best. It is a constant embarrassment

207

for many players to keep asking their boss for yet another afternoon off. Some firms are happy to encourage the sporting prowess of their employees; some firms may actively benefit from having a leading sportsman on their staff who can make contacts all over the world; other firms cannot afford it. Yet there is little acknowledgement of their long-suffering support of rugby. Even the offer of a couple of stand tickets at the next international, or the use of a hospitality box in the south stand, would be a gesture which many firms would be delighted to receive. It would give them a chance to see why their employee needed so much time away from work or the chance to offer a 'different' day out to a valued client.

It is important that the rugby authorities should recognize how much money people are prepared to put into the game, and channel that money in the way they think best. The Rugby Union should appoint a commercial manager whose job it is to ensure that the game's marketability is used to the benefit of everyone. The boot-money scandal is a case in point: it would never have existed if the Union had taken out a contract with one sports equipment firm to become their official suppliers, as they could well have done at any time over the last five years. Such a contract would surely be worth upwards of £50,000 a year and could have gone to reducing the overdraft on the new south stand at Twickenham or to help the game at grass-roots level. Organizing sponsorship of internationals, the use of international grounds and their facilities for advertising and outside functions, are all areas which need a full-time experienced employee instead of the already overburdened union secretary. In this way rugby could still draw up contracts on its own terms, so that the amateur spirit of the game could be preserved, despite the increased 'professionalism' of the administrators. In the same way the amateur game could, long ago, have cut the ground from under the feet of those who would like to bring about a professional tournament in Rugby Union. A world cup is the answer but any and every scheme for such a competition seems to have been rejected out of hand. There has been much talk during 1983 of a professional 'circus' and all the time I have expected the rugby authorities to react positively in some way but they have not done so. There is no evidence, they say, for any of the stories which have appeared in the newspapers. Obviously they will have discussed, among themselves, what kind of threat a 'circus' poses to the amateur game, they may even have formulated a response, but while they continue to turn a blind eye they weaken their own position in the eyes of the players.

It has not helped that they have appeared to take an unenthusiastic view of the international seven-a-side tournament that Cathay Pacific and the Hong Kong Bank sponsor in Hong Kong each March. I was a member of the winning Barbarians VII in 1981 and the whole tournament was an eye-opener. I was amazed to see such a high standard of play from countries who, in the normal course of events, are seldom spoken of in rugby circles in Europe; countries like Thailand, South Korea, Western Samoa. It was a great meeting of rugby-playing people and you could see the sheer delight on the faces of those 'minnows' who suddenly realized that they were to play against the All Blacks, or the Australians, or the Barbarians. The tournament adds a vivid splash of colour to the world scene in what amounts to a world-cup atmosphere and the organization is first-rate, though rugby's establishment has done little enough to make it so. With the Hong Kong sevens as a model, how much more successful might a genuine world-cup tournament be?

It is a source of some concern to me that I have never been asked to play rugby league! I would like to have been able to turn round and say that I had rejected an offer of £50,000 from a league club – my halo would have been shining. Obviously it has been spotted that I am far from the archetypal rugby-league player. Playing Rugby Union for money is a different kettle of fish altogether. I first heard rumours of the possibility of a professional tournament after the 1977 Lions had returned from New Zealand. The general conception then – and a hazy conception it seemed – was that many of the older All Blacks would be involved in a tour of Australasia. When, the following year, Fran Cotton, Billy Beaumont and I were asked if we would like to return to New Zealand, with our wives, to help the Zingari Richmond club to celebrate their centenary, the Rugby Union would not allow it. The by-laws of the game state that such invitations can only be accepted with the Union's blessing. They may have been worried that we would be 'exposed' to temptation. To say we were a little sore about it would be understating the case, particularly when we saw that three of the Scots, Andy Irvine, Jim Renwick and Ian McLauchlan, had been permitted to go. Perhaps Scotland are not as reactionary as they are always labelled. There were one or two whispers at home relating to the professional tournament but no more than that, and I cannot even recall much discussion among the players about it. There was a feeling that one or two of the seventies 'superstars' might have been approached but I heard nothing definite.

In 1983 it was different. Players from all four home countries found themselves being approached direct by David Lord, an Australian sports commentator and agent. I had met Lord when Leicester were touring in Australia in 1980; he was front man for a televised sports programme in Sydney and invited me onto the show for an interview on the club's tour. When he flew to England this year I met him, with Steve Smith, in Manchester to hear what he had to say. He had asked us to meet him and, while we were not placing ourselves on the market, we went with an open mind to hear his suggestions.

The projected professional tournament that Lord was selling has been well publicized. In brief, over two hundred players from all over the world were to be brought together in national squads to play matches at a variety of world venues over a two-year period. To achieve this would cost in the order of £20 million, with each player receiving some £90,000 minimum in exchange for his amateur status. The amount of money required to finance the tournament seemed to me at the time astronomical but, to ensure that the best players would make themselves available, the reward needed to be that high. The amateur game, after all, offers a great deal in terms of travel and experiences well outside the normal realm, so the carrot offered by a professional tour has to be large. What impressed me about the scheme outlined by Lord was that the organizers had gone for national squads so that the players concerned would feel they were still representing their own countries, and so that spectators could identify with the teams. There was no amorphous 'Rest of the World' team, or a European team lacking in national characteristics.

All summer I kept an open mind on the subject. I did not see what Lord was proposing as a threat to the amateur game. The numbers involved are very small compared with the overall number of players available and the anticipated outcome of these proposals would be what many leading players would love to see: the best in the world playing the best in the world, exactly what the amateur game would offer if the International Board approved a world cup. Like a league structure in England, the organization of a world cup becomes simply a matter of administrative detail if the principle is agreed. A world cup would not take the place of the existing international championship once every four years. Instead it could be superimposed on the championship, with world-cup results also counting towards the determination of that season's table. It has been said that a world cup would create extra pressure on players but I do not accept that. Players put up with enough as things stand and if they were working towards what, for many of them, would be the ultimate ambition, they would 'endure' the pressure.

As I write I do not know whether Lord's project will get off the ground. I do know that many players would be interested in both the nature of the competition offered and the money said to be available. They would have to be mighty sure of their ground before they accepted it. Even if the 1983–84 season passes without professional Rugby Union being played, it is my belief that we will see it happen at some stage over the next decade because the popularity of the game is growing so fast and with it its commercial value. Whether that value is directly linked to rugby because it is an amateur sport is difficult to judge. But if enough people, players, administrators and marketing men want to get the professional game off the ground, then all the difficulties will dissolve. The venues will become available wherever there are sports grounds for hire. It would probably be better at first to run a professional tournament at smaller grounds because of the likelihood of attracting relatively small gates. The impact would come from television and the crowds would gradually build up.

There is no reason why a professional tournament, though it might be implemented for money-making purposes, should not remain true to the game and, in that event, there would be no sense of betrayal for players turning their backs on the amateur game. If it worked well – and the 'if' is always a big one in any new venture – it would serve to generate interest in the game as a whole, professional and amateur. You would, in effect, create the sort of team spirit, the feeling of playing for one another, that exists on a Lions tour – which, when you boil it down, is amateur players competing in an amateur game in the most professional way. A professional tournament could take the leading players in the world to countries where they are seen all too infrequently and, conceivably, could serve to improve playing standards. Unfortunately, the rules of amateur Rugby Union as they now stand would not permit the professional players to go as individuals to schools, colleges and junior clubs to talk to and coach the next generation of players.

Professional and amateur Rugby Union could exist

212

side by side, in the same way that professionals and amateurs do in football, cricket and golf. There would be no huge drain of players to the professional game. I can also imagine two reasons which might effectively decrease the likelihood of professional Rugby Union appearing: the institution of an amateur world cup and a relaxation of the rules relating to amateur status which might allow players, for instance, to write books and retain the profits, and which might produce some kind of compensation for the time lost to players absorbed in the highest reaches of the game. Times have changed since the amateur rules were laid down yet the authorities seem determined to preserve the attitudes current when they themselves were players. What they believe in is not necessarily best for the game. The same may be true of the views expressed by today's players, but there must be some common ground between the two sides – if only there was some indication of a willingness to look for it.

Appendix

Name: Peter John Wheeler
Position: Hooker
Playing weight: 13 st 10 lb
Height: 5 ft 11 in
Born: South Norwood, London
Clubs: Old Brockleians; Leicester
Counties: Kent (1969–70); Leicestershire (1970–74)
Barbarians: Debut *v.* East Midlands (1974); eight appearances include Barbarians *v.* Australia (1976) and Barbarians *v.* New Zealand (1978). Selected for Barbarians *v.* Australia (1982) but game cancelled. Member of Barbarians squad for Hong Kong sevens (1981 and 1982). Barbarians tour to Canada (1976)
Representative games: Midland, London and Home Counties *v.* Rugby Union President's X V (1971); Midland Counties *v.* Japan (1973); Midland Counties (East) *v.* New Zealand (1973); Midland Counties (East) *v.* Australia (1975); Midlands *v.* New Zealand (1978); Midlands *v.* New Zealand (1979); Midlands *v.* Australia (1981)
International invitation sides: French President's X V *v.* France (1977, try); England & Wales *v.* Scotland & Ireland (1980); WRU President's X V *v.* Wales (1981); Five Nations X V *v.* Western Province and SA President's X V (1982); Western Province Centenary XV *v.* Western Province (try) and South African XV (try, 1983)
England X V:v. Argentina (1978) 13–13; *v.* Fiji (1982) 60–19

England: 1975 *v.* France 20–27, *v.* Wales 4–20
1976 *v.* Australia 23–6, *v.* Wales 9–21, *v.* Scotland 12–22, *v.* Ireland 12–13
1977 *v.* Scotland 26–6, *v.* Ireland 4–0, *v.* France 3–4, *v.* Wales 9–14
1978 *v.* France 6–15, *v.* Wales 6–9, *v.* Scotland 15–0, *v.* Ireland 15–9, *v.* New Zealand 6–16
1979 *v.* Scotland 7–7, *v.* Ireland 7–12, *v.* France 7–6, *v.* Wales 3–27, *v.* New Zealand 9–10
1980 *v.* Ireland 24–9, *v.* France 17–13, *v.* Wales 9–8, *v.* Scotland 30–18
1981 *v.* Wales 19–21, *v.* Scotland 23–17, *v.* Ireland 10–6, *v.* France 12–16
1982 *v.* Australia 15–11, *v.* Scotland 9–9, *v.* Ireland 15–16, *v.* France 27–15, *v.* Wales 17–7
1983 *v.* France 15–19, *v.* Scotland 12–22, *v.* Ireland 15–25

England tours: Far East (1971): *v.* Waseda University (three conversions) 56–4; *v.* All Japan 27–19; *v.* Singapore 39–9; *v.* Ceylon 40–11
Japan, Fiji and Tonga (1979): *v.* Japan (try) 21–19 (Osaka); *v.* Japan 38–18 (Tokyo); *v.* Fiji 19–7; *v.* Tonga 37–17
Canada and North America (1982): *v.* Canada East (replacement) 52–3; *v.* Canada 43–6; *v.* Pacific Coast 28–6; *v.* Mid-West 58–7; *v.* United States 59–0

British Lions: New Zealand (1977): *v.* Wairarapa-Bush 41–13; *v.* Taranaki 21–13; *v.* Wanganui-King Country 60–9; *v.* Otago 12–7; *v.* New Zealand Universities 9–21; *v.* South and Mid Canterbury-North Otago 45–6 (try); *v.* Wellington 13–6; *v.* New Zealand (second Test) 13–9; *v.* Waikato 18–13; *v.* Auckland 34–15; *v.* New Zealand (third Test) 7–19; *v.* North Auckland 18–7; *v.* New Zealand (fourth Test) 9–10; *v.* Barbarians 23–14
South Africa (1980): *v.* Eastern Province 28–16; *v.* Natal 21–15; *v.* Orange Free State 21–17 (try); *v.*

215

South Africa (first Test) 22–26; *v.* South African Country Districts 27–7; *v.* Transvaal 32–12; *v.* South Africa (second Test) 19–26; *v.* Northern Transvaal 16–9; *v.* South Africa (third Test) 10–12; *v.* Western Province 37–6; *v.* South Africa (fourth Test) 17–13

Captaincy: Leicester 1973–75 and 1978–81; North and Midlands *v.* England (1975) 18–10; Midland Counties (East) *v.* Australia (1975) 11–8; Midlands *v.* New Zealand (1978) 15–20; Midlands *v.* New Zealand (1979) 7–33; Midlands *v.* Australia (1981) 16–10; England *v.* Tonga (1979) 37–17; French President's XV *v.* France (1977); Western Province centenary XV *v.* Western Province 17–22 and *v.* South African XV (1983) 35–37